I'm Still Working on It

A gay veteran's story of overcoming hurt, loss, and PTSD, or at least trying to, anyway.

written by Kevin W. Zalinsky

For Kyle.
For perseverance.
For dealing with your pain in a timely manner and never allowing it
to dictate your life.
For you,
and for me.

Chapter 1:
Queer

I joined the Navy because I walked in on my mom having sex. At that exact, cataclysmic moment in time, my internal monologue probably sounded something like "Oh, my God! Holy shit. What the *fuck*? I have to get out of here." If this were a scene on Cinemax, I'd unplug the TV, cancel my cable subscription, and ready my vows for a life of permanent and irrevocable abstinence. The movies have taught us that the "whole life flashing before your eyes" montage is supposed to play when you're about to die; apparently walking in on your mother having sex isn't much different from impending death. Any meager vestige of my innocence that had managed to survive up until that point disappeared quicker than I could slam the bedroom door in panicked horror.

After scrambling out of the house and frantically calling my sister – who was zero help; she laughed so hard she dropped her phone into the sink – I went on a nice, long walk. I took serious stock of my life: *What am I doing with myself? Is this the place where I belong? Surely I can become the best version of myself anywhere but here?"* I contemplated the terrible things I must have done to deserve such a heinous assault on my psyche: *"Dear God, what did I do to deserve this?"* When I came back to the house, ensuring that enough time had passed that *it* was surely over and done with, I pretended like I hadn't seen a thing, avoided eye contact with her boyfriend, and announced to Mom: "I think I'm gonna go down tomorrow and see about joining the Navy." "Okay, Honey, sounds good," was her chipper response. I don't think Mom was too distraught. In fact, she was positively radiant. Afterglow? Yikes!

My sister Kelly is ten years older than me. She had joined the Navy to escape our mom for completely different reasons. This was your typical "Today on the *Sally Jesse Raphael Show:* Mothers and the Teenage Daughters Who Hate Them," Roseanne vs. Becky stuff. Much less traumatizing and emotionally scarring than my stuff (see above), but this isn't a competition…or is it? Kelly and I often "jokingly" argue over who "gets" Mom when she's senile and completely unhinged. I argue that, because Kelly is the eldest child, it's her inescapable firstborn filial duty to take Mom in. Kelly counterargues that I'm "the Favorite" and therefore Mom is my responsibility. I can't really find fault with her logic – objectively, I *am* the Favorite, being the adorable, freckle-faced, and mostly well-behaved baby of the family. Also, Kelly and Mom drive each other crazy. If I somehow manage to win this one and Kelly gets saddled with Mom, Shady Pines will end up with one more resident to neglect. As the Favorite, that would weigh very heavily on my conscience.

I shouldn't gloat too much, though, since it wasn't much of an ordeal to climb the ranks and attain Favoritehood following in the footsteps of two siblings who so flagrantly and flippantly flounced all over the title. Being the Favorite in my family really just meant being the least terrible. Growing up, from my admittedly limited perspective, Kelly wasn't so bad despite the aforementioned Beckyness. One of my fondest early memories is of Kelly, covered in scrunchies and white denim, singing *Like a Virgin* into a hairbrush in front of her bedroom mirror. A concerned Dad asked an unfazed Mom, "Should we really be letting her sing that?" "Oh, John, it's fine. She's too young to have any idea what it means."

Kelly, being a decade older than I am, didn't really bother with me besides the occasional pat on the head and a "later, alligator" if she happened to glimpse me in the background while AquaNetting her hair in the mirror on her way out the front door. No, Kelly reserved her venom for Kathy, as she almost exclusively referred to Mom. Mom *hated* when her kids got fresh and called her by her first name, in the same way Kelly now hates when *her* kids get fresh and call her by her first name – theirs has evolved into a "Mothers and the Teenage Daughters Who Grow Up to Be Just Like Them" kind of relationship.

Mom got Kelly for an arch nemesis, and I got Kyle. Kyle was like the kid from *Problem Child*, the kid from *The Omen*, and every kid from *Children of the Corn*, all mixed together into one freckled nightmare with a garnish of Beelzebub on top. On the day Kyle was born, birds fell out of the sky, fish floated on the surface of blighted waters, bees entirely lost the ability to navigate, and George H. W. Bush couldn't envision a kinder, gentler America. While other older brothers were ambushing their unsuspecting prey with the classic Noogie, Kyle was double-wrapping my head with duct tape. Aw, was that Atomic Wedgie a little uncomfortable for you? Intrusive underwear is the least of your worries as you're tumbling backwards down a flight of stairs, take it from me. And don't even bother bringing up the Indian Burn! For one thing, that's racist, and second, I'm too busy filling in this eyebrow since Kyle singed mine off with a lighter when I was seven and it still lacks the confidence to fully regrow.

Later in life, I would turn to astrology for an explanation as to why Kyle hated me so much. To my befuddlement, I found it to be chockful of Cancer sympathizing and Aries villainizing: Cancer is cool as water and Aries is blistering as fire; Cancer is sensitive and Aries is brash; poor, overwhelmed Cancer is frightened of Aries! Scared, my ass. Either Kyle managed to slip in under the wrong astrological sign, or he broke the whole damn system when he came hurtling into the cosmos. Upon concluding that astrology is worthless and after checking my daily horoscope, I asked Kelly for her take.

"Kyle didn't *hate* you, Kevin. You were just annoying," she said in that matter-of-fact, holier-than-thou Taurus way.

"Hey! I was *not* annoying," I scoffed. That, of course, is complete bullshit; I'm well aware of how annoying we little brothers can be when we set our conniving minds to it. But still, I argued, in the name of little brotherhood, "How can you take his side?"

"I'm not taking anybody's side. He annoyed the hell out of me, and you, in turn, annoyed the hell out of him. It's the curse of the little brother."

"So who did *you* annoy?" Besides me, of course, since unleashing this torrent of appalling accusations.

"Mom." Kelly smiled smugly. *Such* a Becky.

Sidebar: You'll notice that all three of Mom's kids have names that start with the letter "K." This is not an instance of a racist white lady paying homage to her favorite group of racist terrorists via the first initials of the names of her children, who would then most likely grow up to be racist assholes, too. Mom simply wanted to stick to a theme when naming her kids – That's perfectly normal, right? – and the most obvious theme was "names that start with 'K,' like 'Kathy!'" Poor Dad was the odd man out, but he knew to just let Mom do her thing.

Growing up, we'd pile into the wood-paneled family station wagon, that onetime emblem of working middle class suburbia, and escape the safe monotony of Union, New Jersey for the untamed wilderness of North Carolina for summer vacation. Just one week in the wilderness, though, since Mom and Dad both had to get back to work. But for that one glorious week of blue skies, white sands, clear water free of garbage and syringes, sunset walks on the boardwalk, fishing with Dad, collecting seashells with Mom, SPF 100, popcorn shrimp and hushpuppies, we were New Jersey's answer to *Leave It to Beaver*, or at the very least *not* New Jersey's answer to *Shameless*. I can even see Kyle there in those sepia-filtered memories, showing me how to jump through the waves without getting knocked down, teaching me how to cheat the boardwalk games, giving me giant sand boobs with seashell nipples but *not* covering my face and smothering me. That one week was like the time the Son of Sam took a short break. Now, comparing Kyle to David Berkowitz isn't entirely fair since Kyle never terrorized the world's biggest city with months of brutality, but he also never tried.

The summer after she turned the terrifying age of sixteen, Kelly met *a boy*, which of course led to her sneaking out in the middle of the night, sneaking away from the family in the middle of the day, sneaking under the boardwalk to do things I refuse to imagine, and driving Mom, in her words, up a fucking wall. Mom was always being driven somewhere by us kids, but "up a fucking wall" was probably her least favorite place to be driven. Along the way she was first driven fucking crazy and then driven to fucking drink. Once she was driven up that fucking wall it wasn't easy to coax her down.

On the morning we were set to leave behind the sweet smell of sunscreen and saltwater taffy for the not-so-sweet smell of tri-state smog and sewage, Kelly was nowhere to be found. Thus were Kyle and I gently woken by the dulcet tones of Mom screeching "I'll kill her!" Mom didn't literally kill our sister when she sauntered into the condo at quarter to nine, but not for lack of trying – Kelly was nimbler and slipperier in her youth. At the very least, Mom *did* manage to grab Kelly's arm and send her careening into the wicker furniture like a human bowling ball, breaking her bra strap in the process. In the ensuing chaos of Hurricane Kathy colliding with Tropical Storm Kelly, Kyle and I made our escape for one last visit to the beach. The Incredible Unflappable Dad went about the thankless task of packing up the station wagon as the superstorm raged inside, taking longer drags of his cigarette as "I hate you!" led into "Your ass is grounded!" and "You are such a *bitch*!" gave way to "I brought you into this world, and I swear to God I'll take you out of it!"

"Good morning, Dad!" Kyle and I harmonized in our most innocent voices as we passed. Surely Dad wouldn't stop us from escaping this battlefield?

"You two don't be gone too long, now. We gotta get ahead of that damn traffic." Only three things in this world were ever able to faze Dad: unevenly distributed charcoal which inevitably results in non-uniformly cooked hamburgers; when the balls with the lotto numbers come out upside-down and a winning number 19 is actually a worthless number 61; and that damn traffic.

"Okay, Dad!" Kyle and I trekked down the block to the beach, kicking off our flip-flops when we hit sand. As kids, we'd put our flip-flops on our hands and pretend we were clapping with our feet. On that particular morning, we probably clapped just a little bit louder to drown out the war cries of Zalinsky Deathmatch '94 that hung in the air over an otherwise serene beachside neighborhood.

I discovered something about myself that morning. A lifeguard ran past us as I was on the lookout for treasure left carelessly uncovered and Kyle was on the lookout for boobies left carelessly uncovered. I never paid much attention to grown-ups unless they were giving me allowance or giving me detention for passing doodles in class, but I found myself watching him as he ran by in rippling slow motion. I was paying attention. His hair, and his shoulders, and his arms, and his chest, and his legs, and his leg hair, and his back, and his tanned skin, and his little red shorts – they were all verses in a song of masculinity and virility and sweat that set my little heart aflutter with intrigue and carnality.

"What are you staring at? Don't be *queer*." Kyle pulled the needle off the record of my sexual awakening.

Queer. I had never heard that word before, but I knew instantly that it was a bad word. I didn't have the nerve to ask Kyle what it meant, but I didn't have to: his lips curled into a sneer and his brow furrowed when he said it, as if it were required by law that his face match the unpleasantness of the word. I shrugged it off like a kid might shrug off "nerd" or "loser" or "dumbass," and yet it wasn't shrugged off at all – it was draped across my shoulders, tightened around my neck, dragging on the ground and tripping me up whenever I wasn't paying full attention.

On Sunday mornings, Dad and I had our routine of running errands – "errands" being the hardware store followed by the liquor and lotto store – and organizing the garage. On one such Sunday, after paying a visit to Union Wine & Spirits for Dad's sake and the 7-Eleven Slurpee machine for mine, I asked *the* question:

"Dad, what does 'queer' mean?"

"What? Why are you asking me what that word means?"

"Oh, I…heard it on TV and I wasn't sure. What does it mean?"

"It means…different, strange. Something like that."

"So it means weird?"

"Yeah, it means weird. But we don't say 'queer,' we say 'weird,' okay?"

"So it's a bad word, then?"

"It's just an old word that nobody uses anymore, so if you use it people won't understand what you mean. Just don't say it."

"Okay, I won't say it."

I must have said "queer" a hundred times under my breath after I left the garage. Maybe if I said it enough to myself, its meaning would just implicitly yet fully reveal itself to me, and I wouldn't have to decipher another painfully obtuse adult answer. I hoped that Dad wouldn't give my question a second thought, that he wouldn't realize that I left that conversation much more confused than I was at the outset. Of course, I knew Dad would bring it up at some point to Mom. Mom and Dad talked about everything – the good, the bad, the queer. How that particular conversation went, I can only speculate:

"Your son just asked me what 'queer' means."

"Oh, yeah? One of *my* sons who I had out of wedlock before I met you?"

"Kathy…*Our* son asked me what 'queer' means."

"Alright. So what did you tell him?"

"I told him it means weird."

"I guess it can mean weird."

"He doesn't need to know anything else that it can mean."

"Honey, why does this bother you so much?"

"It doesn't *bother* me. I just don't know where it came from."

"I'll bet you he heard it on that MTV. Those boys watch that *Ben and Stumpy* cartoon and they're always saying wild things."

"*Ben and Stumpy*? Should we be letting them watch a show called *Ben and Stumpy*?"

"Well…How bad can a cartoon really be? But I guess we shouldn't, if it bothers you."

"Kathy, it *doesn't* bother me. His question, I mean, not this stumpy show. I just don't know what an eight-year-old kid needs to know about 'queer,' that's all."

"Honey, it's the Nineties. Things are different now. But you shouldn't be worried that Kevin is—"

"He's an eight-year-old kid, and he doesn't need to know about 'queer,' even if it *is* the Nineties."

I don't know if Dad was worried that, if by asking the question of what "queer" means, I was speaking some self-fulfilling prophecy into being. The word itself was obviously not some kind of catalytic incantation, because I was queer before "queer." I didn't know what "queer" meant, but I *did* know that "queer" meant something to me. As sure as I knew that the sight of that glistening, short-shorted lifeguard galloping along the beach meant something to me. I wonder, did Dad ask himself "Could one of *my* sons really be queer?" How would he have reacted upon learning that the answer to that question is a resoundingly flamboyant "yes?"

Dad and I never had that conversation. I never got to gauge his reaction as I launched into my spiel of "Dad, it isn't a big deal, it's just another piece of who I am, I can't change it, please don't make this weird, I'm still Kevin." I never got to breathe that sigh of relief as he chuckled and said, "I know, Son, now help me move these boxes." Dad, being the good and decent man who I knew and adored, wouldn't have budged an inch in his love for me, that much I know to be certain. But I kept a secret from my best friend, no matter how obvious people assure me it must have been to Dad. Why did I feel the need to keep it hidden from him? Why was I worried that he would respond negatively to it? Did some part of me doubt whether our relationship was strong enough to withstand it? Why do I keep calling my sexuality "it?" Above all else, didn't I know Dad well enough to be sure he'd just chuckle and tell me to get back to organizing the garage?

Chapter 2:
Getting High with Mom

"Oh, Honey, of course you're gay. Remember how we used to watch *Designing Women* together?"

"Yes, Mom. And by the way, *Designing Women* is just a knock-off of *The Golden Girls*."

"Oh, yeah! And *The Golden Girls*! Now, I'm more of a Blanche because I'm like a young, sexy grandmother. Your sister is a Dorothy because she can be mean." Mom was still hurt that Kelly hadn't returned her four phone calls.

"Okay, so you're fine with it, but you're sure *Dad* wouldn't be bothered?" Truthfully, I was never worried about Mom. She encouraged me to dress up as the Wicked Witch of the West for Halloween when I was six. She trilled with delight whenever I'd don her old Dusty Springfield wig and lip sync to *You Don't Have to Say You Love Me*. She'd scoop me up in her arms and plop us down on the couch as soon as she heard "thank you for being a friend" blare out of the TV.

"Honey! Of course I'm sure that your dad wouldn't be *bothered*. Nothing about you would ever *bother* him. You're such a good son. Your dad would be so proud of you. Just look at all that you've accomplished!"

Uh-oh. She was lapsing into Mushy Megaproud Mom Mode. After menopause, Mom had calmed down considerably. She was downgraded from Hurricane Kathy to, at worst, Passing Showers Kathy. Whereas once upon a time she'd express her emotions in a flurry of fury and expletives, nowadays she gets sappy, choked-up and misty-eyed. And it doesn't take much for the waterworks to start, since my mom will brag about her kids to strangers in line at Target.

"Alright, let's get our asses in gear!" Thankfully the expletives are still in active use. "It's Two-for-Five Tuesday!"

"What's Two-for-Five Tuesday?" I hovered my hands near my ears, just in case the answer was sex-adjacent.

"Oh, Honey, it's wonderful! You get two joints for five dollars! But only on Tuesdays. Otherwise it's three for twenty!" She opened her mouth in mock horror, as if she would never pay twenty dollars for weed. "I'll drive, Honey."

My mom drives like a cat behind the wheel, and I don't mean because she has catlike reflexes: she gets easily distracted by sounds, colors, and movements, and whips her entire head in the direction of whatever it was that had grabbed her attention. But, after years of slamming on the brakes at the last possible second because she was so fully invested in whatever story she was telling, Kathy has perfected the Mom Arm Bar: she swings her entire arm in front of whichever kid is occupying the front seat, locks her elbow, and prepares to absorb the entire shock of the ensuing crash. Luckily, her arm has never had to absorb such a force, but forty-two years into motherhood and that Mom Arm Bar is still going strong and fracturing sternums. "Son of a bitch! Did you see the way that guy cut in front of me?"

"Ow!" I checked my ribcage for breaks. "Mom, he had his blinker on for like three cars."

"Well, don't come over so...*stupid!* You know?" She took both hands off the wheel to make the Mom gesture for "stupid" and the car swerved.

"So how did you discover Two-for-Five Tuesday?" I asked, guiding her hands back onto the wheel and sending a little prayer out into the universe.

"Well, I'm retired now...and I'm bored. I'm so bored, Honey. I go to Curves for my thirty-minute workout every morning, I take Dougie for four walks a day, I go to Target, and I get home in time for *The View*. I needed to shake things up a little bit."

"I get it, Mom. I think it's cool that you're opening yourself up to new experiences." Mom would often mention her freshly-coined guiding mantra of "Colorado Calm." Before I saw her in action in the Centennial State, I had assumed Mom was still up to her Jersey Girl antics – flipping people off and screaming at strangers through closed car windows – but she truly had turned over a new leaf, pun intended, in the four or so months since she moved to Denver from New Jersey. "Have you been dating?"

"Yes, I've been dating. But at my age, every guy I meet either has diabetes, or bad knees, or a bad back, or glaucoma, or arthritis, or a really big spare tire. That fat gut is just disgusting to me. These men all fail my basic health check!"

"Don't worry, Mom. You'll find that perfect guy. It's like MeeMaw always said: there's a lid for every pot."

"Well…my mother meant that more like there's a weirdo for every weirdo, Honey."

"You know what I mean! I just don't want you to settle, Mom. You have a lot to offer and your boyfriend should, too."

"Kevin, please. 'Boyfriend?' I'm not fifteen, going to a sock hop," Mom scoffed.

"My bad. I'll call them your 'lovers' instead," I teased her. Mom and I sure have come a long way since that fateful afternoon when I walked in on…well, no need to write it more than once.

"Look, Honey!" Mom excitedly grabbed my arm as a giant fluorescent pot leaf peeked out from behind a Burger King billboard. "The Green Mile!"

"Hey, that's clever!" It was a happy sight, mostly because it meant I had survived another car ride with Mom behind the wheel.

"Hi! Welcome to The Green Mile! My name is Howard! Feel free to browse at your leisure, and please let me know if I can be of any help!" Howard sure was amped up for a guy who spent eight hours a day with joints and edibles.

"Hi, Howard! I'm Kathy, and this is my Honey. He just got out of the Navy after *eleven* years!" She gasped dramatically and grabbed at poor Howard.

"Oh, wow! That's impre—" Howard nearly choked on his tongue when Mom took him by the hands and joggled his arms like wet pool noodles.

"Isn't that *impressive?*" Mom may have cut Howard off, but his brownie-eating grin was plastered firmly in place.

"Hi, Howard!" I broke the two of them up before Mom could dislocate Howard's arms from their sockets. "My *human name* is Kevin and I'd love a quick rundown on all of your wares! Thanks!" The exaggerated excitement was contagious.

"Sure thing, man! Let's start you off with our Blue Dream strain! It has a low THC percentage and offers a nice body high, which is perfect for someone who's just starting out! After you get a little experience under your belt, we can advance you to our Gorilla Glue!"

"Kevin was in *Bahrain*! That's near *Saudi Arabia*! Oh, Howard, I was so worried about him! I haven't slept in two years!"

"I'll take Blue Dream! And it's Two-for-Five Tuesday, isn't it?" I could feel Mom positively radiating pride behind me. That's the one thing that I will always appreciate about my mom, even if it's cripplingly embarrassing most of the time: she's proud of me. She's proud when I serve honorably in the United States Navy for eleven years, and she's proud when I remember to mention that it's Two-for-Five Tuesday so I can score cheap weed at The Green Mile.

I played it safe and went with two joints of the Blue Dream variety, and Mom sprang for the Gorilla Glue and something called "Skunk Berry;" Howard assured her it tasted and smelled like neither skunks nor berries. Mom and I each paid our five dollars and left The Green Mile, but not before Mom and Howard exchanged their Facebook, Instagram, and personal contact information.

"Wow, Howard!" Mom exclaimed after he approved her follow request and she started perusing his photos. "You've got a great eye!"

"Thanks, Kathy! I hope you and your son enjoy those joints! Hit me up the next time you're thinking about coming in! I can give you a sweet discount!"

"I sure will!" Mom waved goodbye as we walked past the security guard. I always tease Mom for talking to everyone everywhere she goes; as a kid, it horrified me and I'd beg her not to talk to strangers. "See, Honey? You make friends, you get discounts. And you always make fun of me for talking to people!"

* * *

"This is happening. I'm about to get high with Mom."

"The trick is to keep your cherry lit. But not *too* lit, otherwise your slow burn will turn into a quick burn. And that's a waste of good green!" Mom was talking like a Food Network host; I was waiting for her to turn to the imaginary cameras and cut to commercial break, but not before teasing a no-bake dessert made only with things found under the kitchen sink. "You want to take a nice, long drag so your fire doesn't go out. Keep that cherry lit!"

"Geez, Mom. You're like the Martha Stewart of weed."

"Oh, Honey," Mom chuckled as she scanned the imaginary studio audience. *"Martha Stewart* is the Martha Stewart of weed. She's been hanging out with that Snoop Doggy Dog for a long time now."

"How do you know these things?" I was flabbergasted. Mom had gone from screaming "Your ass is grass!" when we were in trouble as kids to coolly teaching her adult son how to smoke grass.

"I told you, I'm retired! I have a lot of time on my hands. You'd be amazed what you can find on that YouTube. Now, when it comes to inhaling," Mom took a hit of the joint, shattering the image I had held of her for the entirety of my life, "You want to hold the smoke in your mouth, and then suck it in as you also inhale through your nose. It might burn the back of your throat, so be careful, Honey."

I followed my pothead mom's instructions, and, after a few rounds of choking and sputtering, I successfully and sharply drew the smoke into my lungs and felt the throat burn. I never realized there was so much trial-and-error and bodily discomfort involved in getting high; *That '70s Show* had always made it look so effortless. "There it is!"

"Good job, Honey!" We high-fived and spent the next ten minutes trading our best Bill "I did not inhale" Clinton impressions.

Eventually, our slow burn gave way to the burning question: "Why did he do it, Honey?"

"I don't know, Mom." By this point, my fingers were needling and my teeth had started to go numb as the THC worked its magic. The esophageal burning had thankfully subsided. "I just don't know."

This is the start of a conversation my mother and I have had at least a hundred times in the past eight years. Every single time, I see it coming from a mile away: Mom has such an expressive face that it divulges every little thought, every minor annoyance, every fleeting sentiment. She'll be looking at me, her eyes welling with emotion; she'll sigh as her gaze drifts away for a moment or two; she'll inhale sharply, snapping herself back into the present; and her eyes, finding their way back to my face, are practically bursting with that question: "Why did he do it?" Every time I sense it approaching, I'm filled with dread. Because every time she asks it, I don't have the answer. I don't know why she expects me to have the answer. I don't know why my brother committed suicide. But I don't resent Mom for asking me the same question a hundred times; she doesn't have the answer, either, but she needs it.

"Mom, don't do it," I plead in vain every single time, "Don't blame yourself."

"Honey, I should have sensed that something was wrong." Mom never passes up the opportunity to blame herself for what my brother did.

"How could you have? Kyle didn't let anybody know that he was in a bad place."

"So, you had *no* idea?" Mom leaned in closer and squinted her eyes as she scanned my face, as if she were a middle school teacher asking a kid if he's the one who stuck the "KICK ME HARD" sign to her back and she expected a fib.

"No." That's complete bullshit. Mom was right to suspect that I'd lie, but under no circumstances could I possibly tell her "Well, now that I think about it, there *were* a lot of warning signs." Kyle lived his life without concern for his well-being, without regard for the consequences, without consideration for the future. The red flags were all there, and anybody who wasn't blinded by his charisma could've easily spotted them. But that's the thing about my brother: he dazzled *everyone* with his charm. Everyone except for me, so I have no good excuse. I fastened the blinders myself.

"I just wish he had let me know that he was hurting." Her voice cracked and I braced for water impact. "I was his *mother*."

"I know, Mom. I know." I didn't have a clue. I had no idea how I could possibly comfort her. I lost someone who used to push me down the stairs, burn off my eyebrows, and tell me I had been found wandering out of the woods and it was only a matter of time before my *real* parents came looking for me. Mom lost her firstborn son, and she lost him four years after she buried her husband. With Dad, Mom and I had something in common: we adored that man. With Kyle, it was complicated.

"I'm so lucky that I still have you." Mom grabbed my hand and squeezed, probably to help fight back the tears; I was proud of her for keeping that deluge at bay.

"Yes, you do! And you have Kelly. Don't forget Kelly! You'll have me *and Kelly* for a very long time."

"Yeah, sure." Mom rolled her eyes. "Your sister never answers the phone or returns my calls, but I can always count on her." I am *definitely* getting Kathy when she's senile and unhinged. "I just miss him so much."

"I miss him too," I offered as sincerely as I could possibly muster, knowing the implications if I didn't say anything, or avoided eye contact, or took a long sip of coffee, or, in this exciting and novel case, took a hit of the joint instead. As it turns out, weed doesn't much alter the structure, content, or mood of this eight-year-old conversation.

Of course I miss my brother. It's the strangest feeling when, for twenty-four years, someone in your life occupies the space labelled "only brother," and then, unexpectedly and definitively, it's empty. Kyle left a void in my life – in my heart – that I wasn't aware could exist. I hadn't noticed how much space he took up until it was vacant. I don't miss his cutting remarks, or that look he gave me when I'd breathe too loud – my *respiration* annoyed Kyle – before screaming "Stop breathing so loud, Goddammit!" I certainly don't miss the constant and violent ways he'd announce his presence. But I miss his presence. And I suppose I most miss the potential there was for a better relationship.

I often like to remind Mom of the time I was home on my very first Christmas leave from the Navy. Kyle and I sat at the kitchen table after she and Kelly had said good night and gone up, by this point shoulder-deep in a case of Stella. Maybe it was the serenity of our New Jersey Norman Rockwell knock-off winter wonderland, most likely it was the drunkenness, but we were actually enjoying each other's company. When the buzz was good and our guards were down, we made a promise to each other. A series of promises, to be exact:

"I promise...never to beat you up again," Kyle kicked things off. "Even though you're jacked now and would beat the shit out of me."

"Aw, thanks. I promise to...never again call you an idiot." Kyle nodded approvingly.

"I like that. You have to give me a *little* credit sometimes. Okay, okay. I promise not to call you fat anymore. Mostly because you're not fat anymore."

"And *I* promise not to call *you* stupid anymore."

"Wait a minute. You already promised that one!" Before I could defend my flagrantly duplicate promise, he continued, "Calling me stupid is just like calling me an idiot."

"Hey, I was just checking your intelligence. And you pass!"

"Alright, smartass. Do you have another *real* promise?"

"Yeah, I do. I promise to not roll my eyes when you talk…*as much*."

"Fair enough. So I promise not to give you this supposed 'look' you mentioned. As much."

"It's an actual thing that you do. And thank you. I promise…not to hide in my room if you bring your friends over. I'll try to be friendlier if I see them this time."

"Good! My friends actually really like you, you know. I promise…" Kyle trailed off. He had an uncharacteristically pensive look on his face; I thought the Stella had finally caught up with him. "I promise to be a better brother. You're my only brother, and…I need to be better to you."

I was taken aback. My heart fluttered, for Christ's sake. I fought back any and all signifiers of my joy at having heard such an unexpected sentiment. I certainly couldn't let Kyle know that he had the ability to make me even the tiniest bit happy.

"Well? Don't leave me hanging here! Saying this mushy shit…"

"I…promise to be a better brother, too."

"Sweet. Then it's a deal." We clinked our half-empty cans of Stella.

We stayed up for just a little while longer, silently watching the snow drift past the frosted kitchen window. Mom yelled "You two go to sleep so Santa Claus doesn't skip our house!" from upstairs – she still writes "From Santa" on at least half of our presents – and we obliged, laughing to ourselves as we cleared the crushed cans from the kitchen table and broke down the empty cardboard beer carton.

"Merry Christmas," Kyle and I said to each other from across the hall as we closed the doors to our adolescent bedrooms. I heard Mom sneak downstairs with her plastic Target bags overflowing with presents.

Chapter 3:
Brothers and Other Enemies

One early October afternoon, when I was probably fourteen so Satan was seventeen, my bedroom door flung open and he sprang in. I braced myself for whatever blunt object or verbal assault he planned on bludgeoning me with. Instead, he stood in the doorway, giving me an unprecedented comfortable amount of personal space, and he just looked at me. But not in the usual way Kyle would look at me, where he'd scrutinize everything from my fatness to my freckles to my braces to my hair to my clothes as he worked out the most brutal insult for that particular moment. Something was off; he was *smiling*. And not like a demon clown with sharp, rotten teeth might smile into a baby carriage before feasting on the tears of an infant, either. He was looking me in the face and *smiling pleasantly.*

"What?" I asked pitifully, torn between playing dead and making a futile break for it.

"Come on, let's go."

"Can we just get this over with? I need to finish my homework."

"Get what over with?"

"Just punch me or call me a fatass, already."

"Why would I do either of those things to my only brother?"

"Oh boy. This is some next-level Kyle shit right here," I must have thought to myself as I looked for the nearest escape route. *"Okay, I guess I can throw myself out the window."*

"Seriously, let's go. Dad said I could borrow the car."

My brother drove like a fucking maniac. He'd be lighting a cigarette, checking his hair in the rear-view mirror, texting a girlfriend on his flip phone, and changing out a CD, all at once while going twenty over the speed limit and treating stop signs like they were friendly suggestions. Why Dad would ever let Kyle borrow his brand-new certified used Ford Focus, I'll never understand. Wait, of course I do. Mister Charming, what did I tell you?

"Where is it?" Kyle had his hundred-disc CD case opened in his lap, flipping past the Kinks and Bob Dylan and Tom Petty and U2 until he found what he was looking for. "This is *Exile on Main Street*. This is my desert island album. If anybody ever asks you what my favorite album is, the only correct answer is *Exile on Main Street*. I want you to play this at my funeral, start to finish."

"Is that the Beatles?" I knew full well that it was *not* the Beatles, but I couldn't resist testing out this new-and-improved, kinder, gentler Kyle. He didn't punch me or even call me a dipshit!

"No, Kevin, it's the Rolling Stones. But good guess." Wow, he was really committing to this role.

"Alright, so where are we going?" I was waiting for him to crack, to quit this charade already. I figured the sooner he gave it up, the fewer miles I'd have to walk home after he kicked me out of the car and peeled off while cackling maniacally.

"I just want to go for a ride. And talk."

"Talk about what?" When Kyle wasn't talking about dead Beatles, he was talking about tits. We really didn't have much in common.

As we made our way through those winding New Jersey country roads, I was able to closely examine Kyle as I feigned interest in the changing colors of the leaves. His demeanor was calm yet a little fidgety; his eyes were serene but just the faintest bit bloodshot; his smile, which persisted, twitched every few seconds. The New Jersey Public School System's *D.A.R.E.* Program hadn't failed me: he was *high!* But high on what? At the time, naïve teenage Kevin might have initially assumed pot, but even *he* could have eventually deduced that it was stronger stuff. But what kind of stuff? How did he obtain such stuff? Did he know a drug dealer? Was *he* a drug dealer? I wasn't about to ask any sensitive questions and send him into a murderous marijuana-fueled rage.

…Maybe the *D.A.R.E.* Program had failed me, after all.

"Kevin, you know it's going to be hard, don't you?"

Finally, the time had come. *"Here we go. Yeah, it sure will be hard to walk home from all the way out here. I guess I'll see you tomorrow, asshole."*

"Life is going to be hard for you," Kyle warned, mustering the gravitas of all seventeen years of his worldly wisdom.

What was he getting at? Life hadn't exactly been a picnic up until that point, and he'd only been an entire colony of fire ants stinging my legs and pissing acid into my lemonade. I was getting frustrated with this ordeal. "Kyle, what are you talking about?"

"I know you don't like girls." He said it without the tiniest trace of contempt; his expression remained serene.

"Oh no." Is this the part where I make a floundering attempt to talk about boobs and vaginas and embarrass all present parties, including – and most painfully – myself?

Kyle looked over at me and gauged my reaction, as if he had made a baseless claim and was expecting an indignant argument from my corner. Instead, I countered with cheeks as bright as a freshly-boiled lobster and averted eyes that were *really* into the changing colors of those leaves. He spoke the truth, and maybe, after seven years of struggling with why I felt compelled to look at boys as they looked at their dads' old copies of *Playboy*, I didn't have the energy to argue or to lie.

"You don't. And it's okay." I couldn't stop myself from whipping my head and staring him right in the face. The tone of his voice in that moment was so foreign to my ears. How was it possible for Kyle to sound so understanding, so sympathetic, so *nice?*

"It is?" Is all I could muster.

"Of course it is. You're gay, and there's nothing wrong with that."

"Gay" sounded less offensive, less loathsome than "queer." Kyle hadn't felt compelled to make an ugly expression when he said "gay," after all. Even so, I was uneasy. Kyle said "you don't like girls" and "there's nothing wrong with that," and yet I felt there surely must be. Why else would I have felt so uncomfortable, so out-of-place, so disconnected whenever I was in the company of other boys? I'd squirm as if I'd just committed a crime, as if I were mere moments from being outed and indicted, and they'd proceed to jeer and lob their slurs. For as innocuous as it had sounded when Kyle said it, they could just as easily twist "gay" into a harsh, ugly obscenity. Kyle had me all figured out, and I knew it was only a matter of time before the telltale signs – my soft voice, my effeminate mannerisms, my disinterest in just about everything that occupied the minds of other boys – would out me to everybody else. I wasn't so sure the others would be as cool with it as my brother was.

I was overwhelmed; I was relieved; I was embarrassed; I was elated; I was terrified; I was speechless. All I could manage to do was sit in that car in complete silence, muzzled by the easy acceptance from the most unlikely of sources. If only Kyle would have gotten high and forced me on road trips more often; maybe we could have continued to get to know each other better, and maybe I could have eventually gotten around to saying "Thank you, Kyle. Thank you for being so cool about this, and also for not fashioning this into a scathing dis for your repertoire of insults." After a while, we pulled off the road into some abandoned gas station overrun with weeds, and we sat there, windows down and volume up, as *Exile on Main Street* played from start to finish.

* * *

"Why are her nipples so big?"

"That's what girls' nipples look like, stupid."

"Oh." How did Kyle know what girls' nipples looked like?

"Oh man, look at that *bush*!" Dustin excitedly pointed at the *Playboy* model's, well, *bush* I guess was the best way to describe it. His eyes were as big as her nipples.

"Woah…" Kyle flipped through the crinkled pages of Dad's magazine, seeking out more forbidden wonders of the female anatomy. As he, Anthony, Dustin, and Louis adjusted themselves, I squirmed for an entirely different reason. Luckily, I didn't have to work too hard to convince my brother and his friends that I, too, was interested in Miss March 1973, since all eyes were on her…bush.

"What you think they feel like?" Louis asked, wiping the drool from his chin.

"Balloons filled with warm water," Dustin suggested.

"No way. They have more *heft* to them," Anthony rebutted. "Probably like wet bags of cement."

"They're not always wet, you dumbasses," Doctor Kyle the Sex Expert chimed in, "But I guess it would be pretty hot if they were."

"Yeah!" Louis and Dustin clawed at the pages, their frantic hands colliding.

"What do you think *it* feels like?" Anthony scrambled straight from second base to home plate. That seemed, even to me, like an egregious breach of protocol. Of course we all knew what he meant by *it*, even if our juvenile minds barely had a grasp on our own anatomy. I had no real desire to look at *it*, but I felt my eyes being forced downward by the carnal curiosity permeating the basement workshop where Dad had hidden his stash from the past. My prepubescent gay eyes could handle only so much of Miss March's bare beauty; that stark pink framed by untamed brown was just too much glory to bear.

"I'm gonna go…ride my bike or something."

"What, are you a fag?" Anthony sneered.

I was physically incapable of speaking in the immediate aftermath. My cheeks became flushed and my mouth swung open as if I had forgotten how to control it.

"Well, are you a faggot?" Anthony doubled down, literally, spitting two ugly syllables at me instead of just the one.

If "queer" had slapped me on the cheek, "faggot" gave me a bloody nose. "Queer" made me short of breath; "faggot" stomped on my throat.

Anthony was a shifty, snarky, snickering, *mean* kid. I hear he grew up to be a New Jersey state trooper. I'll bet he's the kind of state trooper who would give a speeding ticket to a panicking husband who's driving ten over the speed limit in order to get his wife, whose water broke a half hour ago and whose contractions are now fifteen minutes apart, to the hospital before she delivers their baby in the front seat of a car. Any negative portrayal of a cop you've seen in film or on television within the past twelve years was probably directly inspired by Anthony. Kyle was loveable doofus Ralph Wiggum in comparison. I had always hated Anthony. I used that hatred as fuel as I pummeled him with my fat little fists, much to the shock and delight of Kyle and his other, lesser asshole friends. Kyle was especially overjoyed, cheering me on in a heartwarming display of brotherly pride. That moment definitively turned the tide of our relationship, forever cementing Kyle as my ally, my confidante, and, above all else, my best friend.

Yeah, right. None of that happened. Anthony continued to leer at me, Dustin howled with laughter, Louis was still busy adjusting himself, and Kyle gave me a look that said, "Just get out of here already." So I did. I had felt like a trespasser, an unwelcome outsider among pubescent perverts. So, gutted yet relieved, I scurried up the wooden basement stairs, yelled "Gonna go ride my bike!" as I raced past Mom starting a pot of coffee in the kitchen, and sprang outside into the fresh summer air. The only bushes out there were the ones Dad was clipping in the front yard. What a relief! "See you later, Son. Tell your little friends I said hi."

Kyle had Deplorables for friends, and I, to quote Dad, had the United Nations. Dad liked to joke that picking me up from a friend's birthday party was like attending a session of the U.N. General Assembly, but at least it was easy to pick me out from the crowd. My best friends were Emma, Georgie, Martin, and Aesha. Once, some jerk with a rattail and a permanent scowl snapped, "Hey kid, don't you know you're white? White kids are supposed to hang out with white kids, dumbass!" to which Emma replied "Kevin ain't white! You see all those freckles?" None of us had any doubts as to my whiteness, but we bonded not over something as superficial as skin color, but rather the important things: knock-knock jokes, bike rides, kickball, Saturday morning cartoons, catching up to the ice cream truck, and playing outside all day until the voices of five moms announced, in near-perfect synchronization, "Dinnertime!"

Our coalition stood strong in a unified front against the evils that plagued our precious third grade world: Georgie was the smartest kid at Franklin Elementary, Martin knew all of Union's hidden byways and back ways, Aesha would never shy away from telling on someone to the highest authority, I was a good fifty pounds heavier than the next biggest kid in class, and Emma had a mouth that would make a knuckle-tattooed sailor blush.

"Fuck them!" I could always count on Emma to say just the right thing. She lived right down the block; we met up and rode our bikes to Biertuempfel Park a few streets over. Anytime we'd go to the park, we'd make a beeline straight for the swing set, and my swing would hang just a little closer to the ground.

"They were acting so weird," I told Emma, shaking my head in bewilderment. "I was really uncomfortable."

"I woulda been too, looking at naked people! Those guys are fucking gross."

"Yeah, that is pretty gross, right?"

"How did you get roped into that shit, anyway?"

"I don't know. Kyle wasn't being as big of a jerk this morning. I thought we were gonna play Pogs or something. It wasn't so bad until Anthony showed up."

"Man, *fuck* Anthony! *And* his sister's a real bitch. It's gotta run in the family."

"Probably. His parents look mean, too." Anthony's mom originated Resting Bitch Face and his dad's brow was perpetually furrowed. They always seemed to be a deeply unhappy couple, which might have explained their deeply unpleasant children.

"Don't let it bother you too much. You don't need to be looking at naked ladies with those assholes in the basement, anyway. Just hang out with me!" Emma grinned, showing every tooth in her mouth in that great big cheesy way she smiled whenever she wanted to cheer me up.

"I don't really care about them. But Anthony called me a faggot."

"Are you serious?" If it were possible for a swing to come to a screeching halt, Emma's would have. "That's, like, a *really* bad word."

"I know it is. And the way he said it…"

"He's *such* an asshole. You just can't say that word! One time, Junior said that when he was in a fight with some kid – and that kid was a jerk and he started the fight, by the way, so Junior wasn't the bad guy – so Junior called that kid *that*, and when Mom found out about him using that word, not the part about him getting into a fight, well, she gave Junior a whooping and grounded him. That's when I knew you just *can't say*…you know, *that*."

"Yeah, but Junior isn't anything like Anthony. I'm sure he didn't know that you just *aren't* allowed to say it…to anyone. He probably doesn't even know what it means. Anthony definitely knows what it means but he said it anyway. And he said it *twice*."

"Don't take it personal, Kev. He's just an asshole." Emma resumed her usual swinging pace. "Are you gonna tell Mr. and Mrs. Z?"

29

"No way! I can't tell my parents. Kyle would beat the crap out of me. And Anthony would, too, the next time he saw me. You know he jumps kids behind school."

"Fucking *jerk*. Maybe I'll ask Junior to jump *him*." Emma flashed that cheesy grin again. "Bet he wouldn't say, you know, *that*, ever again."

Emma was such a good best friend. I could tell her all about this humiliating episode and just know she'd be on my side the second I mentioned Anthony. She also knew – or maybe the thought hadn't even crossed her mind – not to ask *why* Anthony had felt compelled to call me a faggot. It's a word you just don't use, and that's that. The *why* was irrelevant, but the *who* in this case just so happened to be her best friend, and the members of Franklin Elementary's Model United Nations stood together always in the face of adversity, especially when adversity took the form of a lowdown, ruthless, slur-spewing middle school bully.

I didn't have the words back then to articulate how I felt. I could feel my face getting hot, I could feel the knot welling in the back of my throat, I could feel my skin crawl, I could feel my entire body tense up. But I didn't know what it was that I *felt* as I was getting leered at and laughed at while my brother, who had blindsided me the year prior with another loaded word, stood idly by. Was I ashamed? Was I disgusted? Was I afraid? Was something wrong with me? How is a little gay kid supposed to feel when he's called a faggot?

Growing up, I recall the ranks of homosexuality were, in ascending order of revulsion, "gay," followed by "queer," and then "fag," and finally – and there is a distinction here, however slight the difference between the two words may be – the ultimate insult: "faggot." It was always barked viciously as by a nasty junkyard dog; it was never said casually or in jest; it was never directed at a friend, even in the throes of a volatile adolescent flare-up; it was used, on the cutthroat recess scene, only to shame, humiliate, belittle, dehumanize, and ostracize. Anthony had breached protocol in the same way he ran straight across the field from second base to home plate: he bypassed "gay" and "queer" entirely. "Fag" and "faggot" dripped with venom. He snarled those words and spit them in my face, leaving me stammering and cowering with no option but to run away. I couldn't very well stay and fight. They'd all howl "Kevin wants to *do* you! Don't let him touch you with his faggy hands! Cover your butthole!" I'd be pummeled first with humiliation, second with fists. I wonder, would Kyle have defended me?

Chapter 4:
India

In India, everything was *damp*. Even the carpet in the hotel room was clammy; it felt like I was sloshing through a film of lukewarm bathwater as it stuck to my every footstep. The water poured out of every single pore and drenched my clothes, right down to my socks and undies. I had to apply deodorant every half hour because it would get swept away by a torrent of sweat within a matter of minutes. A brackish waterfall constantly seeped out of my forehead and cascaded down my arms and legs, pooling in the unlucky sneakers which I hope some poor, unsuspecting Indian man at least aired out before pulling on.

Have you ever been on the elliptical, or maybe the Stairmaster, and a bead of sweat dripped onto your iPod Touch, so you wiped it on the shoulder of your shirt – you forgot to bring a towel in this scenario – only to realize that your shirt was drenched in even more sweat, so then your iPod Touch had a film of sweat on its entire screen, and it started frantically pausing, playing, and skipping tracks because it was confusing that film of sweat for your fingers which just couldn't decide on one goddamn command? Well, that's life in India. Just listen to an analog radio. Bollywood music is actually very good.

I'd step out of the hotel room and be immediately enveloped in a thick cloak of humidity. With every step and every swing of the arms, it felt like I was trudging through soup. After a few days, I had learned to maneuver with this muggy phantom wrapping me in its sweltering embrace. India smelled so incredibly sweet: the lotus flowers and curries and spices and, yes, sweat all mingled into a syrupy mélange that hung in the air over the bowl of soup. Every so often, a breeze would cut through the wall of humidity just as easily as it might push vertical blinds in a condominium out of its way. And in those moments, when the cool, sweet breeze would waft by and just barely graze my sticky skin: Nirvana. All other times felt like the seventh circle of Hell. That's the one with the river of boiling blood and fire. Get it? Hot.

As hot and sweaty and *damp* as I remember India being, it remains firmly in the top three foreign countries that I've been fortunate enough to visit. The scenery, the people, the music, the food. Oh, Annapurna, the food! If I wasn't bitching about how hot and wet I was, I was eating. That constant sweat cleanse was exactly what I needed between the tikka masala, and roti, and samosas, and biryani, and gulab jamun, and tandoori chicken, and papadums, and chana masala, and raita. Please Google the nearest Indian restaurant and order all of these things right now; trust me, this book isn't nearly as good.

I was eating, I mean *working*, for a week in India. At the time, my squadron was deployed to Japan, and I was chosen to go sweat it out in India for a short work assignment. The Navy put me up in a first-class, five-star resort; I shared Paradise with wealthy Europeans and got fat on room service. Paradise just so happens to be surrounded by Goa, where garbage literally piles up into small mountains which barefoot kids scale in search of the room service scraps that were picked over and discarded by rich European fatties and an ersatz American fatty.

It was in Goa, on one of my walks from the resort to the nearby Indian Navy base, where I met Arjun. My supervisor had stipulated that I walk to work using only the side streets that zagged through the single-story shanties and four-story trash heaps which surrounded the resort. In his futile attempt to keep me inconspicuous, he forbade me from walking along the paved two-lane highway which provided the direct route. As if a humongous, white, obviously American military man lumbering through a poor little village of Indians is inconspicuous. "You can walk on the highway when you leave work at night, so you don't get raped or murdered." Such a considerate boss.

So, trespass through their humble neighborhood I did, acutely aware of both the smooth, clean road overhead which led directly to the front entrance of my destination, and the *stares*. And the harder they stared, the deeper I sank into the mud. The roads weren't muddy because it had rained recently; they were muddy because of the *damp*. I sweat onto the sweaty roads until we were as one: a sweaty, lumbering, humongous, conspicuous mass of sludge lurching through the humidity and garbage.

I had become a one-man traveling cabinet of oddities and curiosities. As I struggled to make my way quickly through their burb, I attracted quite the following of locals. Mostly children, pointing and giggling, until I'd smile at them and they'd jump away from me as if I were a filthy leper, which was at least half-true: every step sent mud splattering onto the lower two-thirds of my sweaty body. They were all shirtless and barefoot, which made it easy for them to somersault around me, careful not to make contact with my sweat or leprosy. As I rounded an almost comically narrow corner, children ricocheting around me like giggling bullets, I walked into the ass of a cow.

No, really: this cow's ass was staring me right in the face, brown eye to brown eye. It swept its tail from side to side and I screamed internally when I thought cow shit had hit me in the face, before I realized it was just the flies. There were *so many flies*. I had apparently stumbled onto the set of the revival of *The Amityville Horror* and won the coveted role of the sweaty priest covered in flies. I was sinking into the mud as if it were actually quicksand, flies were pecking away at my head, and a cow's udders were warbling in my face; if Hindus believed in Hell, *this* would surely be it.

Suddenly, I felt tiny hands pull me out of the mire and deposit me onto a stone slab. I swept the remaining flies from my face and turned to look upon my pint-sized hero; surely it was a cherub, sent from on high? He was probably seven years old. He had bright, mischievous eyes, a round, happy face, and a huge ear-to-ear grin that proudly showed off all five of his teeth. What was most striking about him, however, were the freckles clustered on the tops of his cheeks and the bridge of his little button nose. He looked like *Kyle!* Whereas I have freckles on virtually every square inch of my body, Kyle had freckles only on the tops of his cheeks and the bridge of his nose. And while Kyle's face slimmed down with age – again, the opposite of me – as children we shared the same round face and chubby cheeks as this tiny toothless angel. Add a few dozen drops of melanin to a base of aggressive Irish pastiness, and I could have sworn that I was staring into the face of my brother's doppelganger. I could hardly believe my eyes.

"Thank you!" I didn't know how to say that in Hindi, but the look of exuberant gratitude on my face surely transcended all language. This boy had only rescued me from the ass of a cow.

"Okay," was his chirpy response. He squinted his eyes, scrunched up his nose, and made some kind of kissy noise. This kid was the definition of "fucking adorable."

"Whew," I breathed a sigh of relief and stood up, adjusting my mud-caked shorts. My new friend swung his arms wildly and shouted commands in Hindi, sending my giggling entourage scattering like flies on the wind. Even the cow moved its ass out of the way.

"Okay!" He grinned, showing off those pearly whites and gummy gums. He pointed at a plywood door behind me, and only then did I realize that the stone slab was actually something of a front porch. I stepped off the porch and positioned myself so that my back wasn't facing the door to this strange hut.

"Oh?" I pointed dumbly at the door. I wasn't about to touch that damn door, much less open it. My friend brushed past me and opened it himself, and then gestured for me to enter. He grabbed me by the elbow when he sensed my obvious hesitation. "Oh."

"Go." This kid was adamant about getting me into this shack.

"Go? Well…" I figured if I hadn't already died from dehydration or whatever bacteria was making the mud smell like that, I should be fine. So I went. "Okay."

Inside I found a single windowless room with walls and a ceiling of more plywood. Sunlight streaked in through cracks in the plywood, so windows weren't necessary; the only view would be a fly-covered cow's ass, anyway. The floor was, thankfully, dry dirt with five or six single panels of cardboard which I assumed were used for sleeping. In the corner was a tea kettle heating up on a hotplate; I knew it was turned on because the smell of burnt metal permeated the tiny room. Tending to the kettle was an old woman squatting with her back to me. All I could muster when she half-turned to look at me was "Hi, ma'am."

She stood, her knees and ankles creaking. She hobbled over to me, adjusting the orange scarf which had been loosely laid on her head. She obviously hadn't been anticipating company. I was fully expecting to be berated in Hindi and beaten by this old woman until I fell backwards into the mud. Instead, when she was within striking distance, she turned her round face up towards me and smiled. I then saw exactly where my young friend had gotten his happy, gummy smile.

"Arjun!" Grandma called, and my friend ran from out behind me and stood beside her; they were about the same height. I can only assume that "Arjun" was my friend's name, because his little ears perked up every time Grandma said it, and also because I'm ignorant and assuming things. Nevertheless, Arjun is a real name – I Googled it – so let's just go with it.

Grandma and Arjun exchanged a few words and she patted him affectionately on the head with her crooked fingers. He ran over to the hotplate and went about pouring a few glasses of tea. Grandma and I could do little but stare at each other. Her toothless smile was so endearing that I couldn't help but smile back. Arjun came back with two small glasses of tea, the first for Grandma and the second for me. The boy was obviously such a good grandson and it warmed my heart to see it.

Speaking of warm, *holy shit* was that glass hot. I could feel my fingerprints fusing with the molten glass fibers. I checked out Grandma's fingers – maybe they weren't crooked but actually shriveled up from holding scalding hot glasses of tea. She threw back that tea like a sailor with a free shot of tequila. My throat hurt just watching it. Still, I couldn't be rude: I was a guest, after all – a guest in a plywood shack in the middle of an unfamiliar neighborhood and I couldn't rule out murder just yet no matter how lovely Grandma seemed – so I pursed my lips and took a tiny bird sip of tea.

"Delicious!" It was, even if the outer layer of my lips was probably floating in the glass. Grandma beamed; she and Arjun had matching ear-to-ear gummy grins. As I politely sipped away at the tea – Grandma had four more shots as I worked on my one – and my hand had gone completely numb, I observed Arjun and became increasingly amazed by the uncanny resemblance. Not only did his face greatly remind me of Kyle's, but the way he zipped around the room like a caffeinated squirrel with ADHD brought me right back to childhood at 1280 Glenn Avenue.

If I only I had been able to say "You look just like my brother!" in Hindi. "Okay" seemed to be the extent of Arjun's mastery of the English language, so talking was pretty much out of the question. Instead, Grandma, Arjun and I spent the next few minutes looking and smiling at one another, with the occasional nervous chuckle from me to spice things up. When it came time for me to leave, I very awkwardly announced "Well, I have to go to work now!" slowly and loudly, as if Arjun and Grandma would magically be able to understand English if it were screamed at them in an obnoxiously slow cadence. They first exchanged a confused glance before smiling back at me, and only when I began waving goodbye in an exaggerated full-arm swing did they understand that I was leaving their home.

I would stop by and visit Arjun and Grandma – and burn off each subsequent layer of my lips until there were only translucent flaps left – every day for the remainder of my week in India. Arjun would be waiting for me on the front porch, swinging a stick like a sword, or throwing rocks at the hut across from his, and yell "Okay!" as soon as he saw me round the bend. With each trek through the neighborhood, I became increasingly better, or at least decreasingly inept, at navigating the muddy alleys and would be less and less exasperated by the time I'd reach him. He'd wrap his lanky arms around my waist in a side hug and lead me into the hut by the elbow every time.

Grandma would act as if her long-lost prodigal grandson had returned to her whenever I'd enter. She, too, would wrap her arms around my waist in a side hug, but not before adjusting the collar of my shirt with her crooked fingers. She reminded me so much of my own MeeMaw; it truly felt like I was with family. Except my biological family talks – *a lot*. But the language barrier, or language vacuum, had no negative bearing on our joyous daily reunions.

Halfway through the week, I got sick. I must have eaten something; well, I ate *a lot* of somethings, but one of those many somethings vehemently opposed its new surroundings. I was, unbelievably, even sweatier than usual. My skin was gray and translucent. I'd open my mouth and smell death on my breath. Anytime I'd foolishly let something pass my lips – plain white bread, water, air – it would violently erupt from my body like hot lava. Think of the bridal shop scene in *Bridesmaids*; thankfully I never had to relieve myself in a sink or the middle of the street. Anyway, one late morning when I stopped by, cheeks fully clenched and sweat pooling on my upper lip, Grandma took one look at me and muttered "Oh…" She hobbled over to her hotplate station, pulled *something* out of a drawer, and crushed it up into a glass of tea. Within minutes of drinking the tea, the ruddy complexion returned to my cheeks, the lip sweat evaporated, and my cheeks unclenched – gone was the fear of soiling my shorts and, by extension, my sweaty legs.

"Oh, wow…Thank you! I was so worried I was going to shit myself!" I exclaimed in my uncensored exuberance. Grandma just smiled and nodded her head. Arjun giggled; did he know "shit?"

On my last full day in Goa, I stopped by the resort gift shop and bought something I thought Arjun would enjoy. I actually bought one of two things that I could afford, but what use does a seven-year-old Indian boy have with a hair clip in the shape of a pineapple? I opted instead to buy him the hand-painted wooden carving of an elephant. It was no karate-chopping, high-kicking action figure with battery-powered limbs, but at least it wasn't a pineapple hair clip. I tucked the tissue paper-wrapped elephant inside my backpack, on top of my work uniform. I knew Arjun would come sprinting up to me and tackle me with a hug as soon as he laid eyes on me, and I didn't want to be fumbling around in my bag and risk dropping his present in cow shit. As it turns out, I didn't have to worry about the cow shit. Besides the smell, of course.

Arjun wasn't there. "*No big deal.*" I thought he must have been inside, getting the tea ready to sear off the last remnants of my fingerprints. I knocked on the plywood door. No response. "*No problem,*" I said to myself. "*It takes Grandma a while to stand up out of that squat.*" A few minutes passed. Kids went sprinting and tumbling up and down the alley, like on any other day, but no Arjun. A few more minutes passed. "*At this point, we're practically family. I'll just let myself in.*" Empty. The pieces of cardboard were all there, the kettle was there, the small glasses were stacked next to the hotplate, and the air smelled faintly of burnt metal, but nobody was home.

I waited for about fifteen minutes. Maybe they went to the market, or maybe for a stroll around the garbage heaps. Except Grandma didn't like to go outside at midday, when I'd walk to work, and Arjun was told to play in front of the hut and not stray too far. These were things I had managed to infer during our week of visits. Eventually, I had to leave. I unwrapped the elephant and laid it at the foot of the cardboard slab which I assumed was Arjun's – it had Iron Man and SpongeBob stickers on it. I turned my cellphone off and returned it to the front pocket of my backpack. I had planned on taking a picture of Arjun and sending it to Kyle as soon as I had WiFi access. "Twins!" the caption would read. I would then take a selfie with Arjun and Grandma as a memento of my own. But I wasn't able to take those pictures. I took one last look at that tiny, windowless plywood room and closed the door behind me.

Work was over that night at around eleven forty-five. As I walked back to the resort on the paved highway, I peered into the abyss beyond the dim traffic lights which dotted the road at random, insufficient intervals. Only inky darkness; no hyperactive little kid racing towards me. I listened for Arjun's jubilant "Okay!" whenever I'd walk through a pool of pale yellow light. I heard only palm leaves rustling in the warm night air and the occasional lemon sputtering by behind me. I couldn't see him and I couldn't hear him, so I imagined him, gummy grin and all, finding that crummy carving of an elephant at the foot of his bed and exclaiming "Okay!"

Chapter 5:
MeeMaw

Close your eyes and imagine, if you will – well, first read the rest of this sentence and then close your eyes and imagine – the sweetest, cutest, littlest old lady you can possibly conjure up. Now that your eyes are open again, I can reveal that the woman you just saw is, in fact, my MeeMaw. Was her bluish-silver hair done up in the most adorable little perm? Was she wearing a pink sweatshirt with a big-eyed kitty cat, or maybe a smiling sunflower, on the front of it? Was she also wearing a pearl necklace, pearl earrings, and too much rouge for no reason in particular other than she was running low on half-and-half and had to run to ShopRite? I told you – MeeMaw.

During the summer before I joined the Navy, and after I had walked in on *you know* – which MeeMaw knew nothing about; I told her I was joining the Navy for all those stereotypical, jingoistic, wholesome reasons the Greatest Generation loves to hear – I spent a lot of time with MeeMaw. I'd visit her at least twice a week. She was in her mid-eighties at the time, and I had no idea when I'd be able to see her again once I got on that bus for boot camp.

We watched a lot of *Judge Judy* together that summer. MeeMaw delighted in hearing Judy's squawks of "Baloney!" and pearls of sage wisdom such as "Don't pee on my leg and tell me it's raining!" and "Beauty fades, dumb is forever!" During the last commercial break of the second episode – *Judge Judy* is on every weekday from four to five p.m. EST, in case you're interested in reveling in an hour of schadenfreude five times a week – MeeMaw would hobble over to the kitchen and get supper in the oven. Supper was usually some kind of casserole or some kind of loaf, always with a vegetable medley and pumpernickel bread smothered in Land O'Lakes butter. By the time the teaser for the evening news was over, MeeMaw was back in her recliner for Judy's final verdict of the day.

The news would be over by the time we'd finish dinner; then came time for an hour of *Jeopardy!* and *Wheel of Fortune.* Every single time I'd manage to correctly answer a 100-dollar question – the lowest tier and typically some kind of timely pop culture reference – MeeMaw would gasp in delight and tell me *"You* should go on this show, Sweetie!" If I'd solve a puzzle after Pat announced that only vowels remained and every letter except for "A" and "Z" had already been called, MeeMaw would still ask "Have you seen this episode already?"

MeeMaw made me feel *special* whenever I visited her. She made all sixteen of us grandkids, and all five of her great-grandkids for that matter, feel *special.* I'd help her with some menial task – reaching a high shelf and getting a decorative vase down, carrying a case of water in from the trunk of her car – and she'd act as if I'd re-shingled the roof or renovated the basement, full bath and all. It wasn't easy leaving MeeMaw behind. I'm sure a part of me figured that she might not be there the next time I was home, but that part was buried under eighteen years' worth of homemade chocolate pudding, extra helpings of casserole, and MeeMaw hugs.

The MeeMaw I imagine has rouge on her cheeks, her permed hair is immaculate, her sensible flats match her sweater. She has tissues in one pocket and hard candies, probably Werther's Originals, in the other. She has a smile for every soul she encounters. Every word she utters is said without a trace of sarcasm, or rudeness, or malice. There is never a backhanded compliment or an ulterior motive. She lives thoughtfully, prays sincerely, and loves unconditionally. You might think, "She sounds like such a sweet old lady," and she was, in fact, such a sweet old lady.

Every time I'd visit her, I'd ask MeeMaw, "Do you want to go see Pop-Pop?" MeeMaw never turned down an opportunity to go see Pop-Pop. I'd offer to drive into town – Hampton, New Jersey, once a bustling railroad town known as "the Junction" between Newark and the small towns beyond, now a sleepy little hamlet of no more than fifty – to St. Anne's Catholic Church where Pop-Pop is buried. But first, MeeMaw would lead me on a tour down memory lane.

"That house there is where the McGillicuddies lived. They were nice enough people, I suppose, but your Pop-Pop hated whenever someone would ask if he was related to them. He'd say, 'I'm a McCormick, and don't you forget it!'

"There's the firehouse where your Pop-Pop worked after he stopped delivering for Coca-Cola. You know, they put up a very nice little plaque for him on the outside of the station after he passed away. There! Did you see it, Sweetie?

"There's the old Dairy Queen. Do you remember, Sweetie? Sometimes I'd pick you up from school and we'd go get an ice cream cone and sit up on the hill there? That was always nice. I used to enjoy sitting there with you as you told me all about your day at school.

"And that's the salon where I get my hair done every Friday. The girl who does my hair is named Virginia, but everybody calls her 'Ginny' for short. I remember when you were little I'd say, 'I'm going to see Ginny to get my hair done' and you'd ask, 'Jenny? Who's Jenny?' and I just got such a kick out of that. Ginny still jokes about changing her name to 'Jenny!'"

The tour would conclude at St. Anne's. After MeeMaw went inside to light a candle and say a prayer for every solitary person she knew, dead or alive, we'd visit Pop-Pop in the cemetery. The McCormicks and Deans, MeeMaw's family, had an entire section of the graveyard to themselves, where I'm sure they laughed, reminisced, carried on, and disturbed their neighbors' rest all day long.

"Hi, Patrick. How are you doing?" MeeMaw's voice broke every time she asked Pop-Pop how he was doing. Every time she approached that headstone was like the very first time since she laid her one true love to rest. "I brought Kevin with me today. He's going to be joining the Navy here shortly. He's going to do very well, don't you think?"

Claire and Patrick met after the war, when Patrick returned from Bad Nauheim and became a driver for the Coca-Cola Company. He was making a delivery to Alice's Five-and-Ten, where Claire had started working the summer after her junior year of high school, and he laid eyes on, if you were to ask him, "the most beautiful girl in the whole darn world." He decided immediately upon seeing her that he'd marry her one day, like a scene straight out of a black-and-white classic in which an impossibly handsome solider-turned-delivery man with immaculate hair makes such a claim without a hint of sarcasm. If you haven't seen that one, I don't want to spoil it for you, but – they get married in the end.

MeeMaw and Pop-Pop were married for fifty-seven years. Even as an otherwise clueless kid at their fiftieth anniversary party, I might have thought "Holy shit, that's a long time to be with one person." It sure is, but Patrick and Claire McCormick took what could have become, for any other couple, a matrimonial life sentence without chance of parole and turned it into the ultimate relationship goals trending on Facebook. They didn't even need a filter for their love story. It's another classic: boy goes off to war, boy kills Nazis, boy's hair is impeccable while killing Nazis (Did Rosie the Riveter find time to air-lift hair gel to our boys in Normandy?), boy comes home alive, boy meets prettiest girl in the whole darn world, boy marries girl.

"Back in those days, a girl just married a fella if he seemed nice and looked okay," MeeMaw would explain to me. "Of course, a girl just couldn't say no to a fella with hair like that!" MeeMaw swooned over Pop-Pop's hair even after it had turned gray and became unkempt with the onset of Alzheimer's.

"Wasn't it hard to be married for so long?" I have difficulty committing to a person for two months, and that's with four personal days a week and every other weekend off. The idea of rolling over in the morning and looking at the same face every day for fifty-seven years is as incomprehensible to me as calculus, and I barely survived long division in the third grade, so you can imagine the bewilderment in my voice when I asked MeeMaw.

"Hard? No, Sweetie. The Depression was hard. Rationing was hard. War was hard. Marriage wasn't hard." MeeMaw never lectured us, or bemoaned kids these days and their Gameboys and their MTV and their silly, insignificant problems. She simply spoke her truth: marriage wasn't hard for her.

If the idea of being married for fifty-seven years to someone who seems nice and looks okay is a relic, well, at least it's a quaint snapshot into a simpler time of rampant Nazis, unchecked racism, dangerously lax drinking and driving laws, and an unopposed heteronormative worldview. *"Times were different,"* I'd assure myself as I questioned whether I'd ever know a love as true – if not as long – as MeeMaw and Pop-Pop's. I counted by tens to figure out how old I'd be in fifty years. Eighty? Yikes! Better find me a dashing hunk and fall head over heels in all-consuming love, quick-like.

Of course times have changed. Nowadays, the filter you pick for your Facebook profile picture is way more important than what you say or even how you look when you meet in person after three days of flirting and emoji-winking on Tinder. "This one makes my teeth look really white, but it also makes my eyes look like raisins." "This one really brings out my eyes by enlarging them to three times their actual size, but now my cheekbones have collapsed into my face." "My profile picture only has thirty-seven likes?! He'll investigate and learn that I only have 709 Facebook friends!" "He only has 709 friends? What's wrong with him? Was he homeschooled?" I can actually count my true friends on two hands; those other 703 people are just padding for my fragile ego so I can delude myself into thinking that I'm much cooler and way more important than reality would otherwise truthfully suggest. "Do you have Snapchat? What's your Insta? How many followers do you have on Tumblr? Has a celebrity ever Retweeted you? Are you *still* on Facebook? That's cute; my parents are on Facebook." It's fucking exhausting.

But if the prospects of finding true love in this digital age are staggering in their improbability, the idea of having children as a gay man with a committed partner is like finding a filter that beautifies your teeth *and* your eyes in your profile picture, which is then "liked" by upwards of a hundred people. The pressure of needing to spawn six kids, sixteen grandkids, and five great-grandkids is crippling. Luckily for me, I was absolved of that responsibility the moment I played my gay card. If *Modern Family* has taught us anything, it's that even a white upper-middle class gay couple can afford exactly one child through adoption or other means, and *maybe* twins if there's a two-for-one deal. The straight siblings in that modern family are on the hook for multiplying the progeny, while the gays and their kid(s) are free to be their quirky, sassy, absolved selves.

So, there's hope yet that I may one day be able to raise a human being and – hopefully – avoid irreversibly screwing them up during the growing process. Still, finding a love worth rolling over for every day for fifty-seven years is at the forefront of my mind – even more important than choosing the perfect filter for the perfect profile picture for the perfect online identity. I'd even settle for waking up in separate beds in separate rooms and mumbling "morning" to each other as our shuffling paths cross in the hallway. At least in that scenario our dentures wouldn't have to float in the same glass.

"I just know you'll find a nice young lady for yourself, Sweetie," MeeMaw had assured me. "What girl could possibly resist such a handsome sailor?"

"Yeah, MeeMaw, I will." That was the only time I had ever lied to MeeMaw in all of our eighteen years together. She was from a sepia world of fifty-year marriages of nice fellas to nice girls, and I – for reasons of convenience or cowardice – chose not to bear the burden of disclosing that life wouldn't always amount to a cookie-cutter love story as enacted by Humphrey Bogart and Lauren Bacall. Sometimes Humphrey falls in love with James Dean and Lauren fools around with Katharine Hepburn.

I was unfair to MeeMaw. I did her a disservice. I had assumed that, because she was eighty-six years old, she'd have a negative opinion of her grandson's homosexuality. I had decided that she was from a bygone era, that she didn't want or need to hear about how times had changed. Most regretfully, I denied her from knowing me fully. I'll never know if she would have gone to Ginny and asked for a rainbow perm for Pride weekend, or if she would have recorded *RuPaul's Drag Race* and sent me the VHS tapes in a care package when I deployed, or, in the most likely scenario, if she would have said "Kevin, you know God loves you no matter what, because he made you and you're perfect just the way you are." I'll never know those things, but I'll always know that my favorite summer of all time included early bird suppers, mostly wrong *Jeopardy!* answers, and a lot of Judge Judy.

"I'll write you every week you're in boot camp, Sweetie," MeeMaw promised, and you'd better believe she wrote me every single week.

Boot camp wasn't difficult, per se, but it was aggressively and mind-numbingly monotonous. I was in a division of one hundred recruits – fifty men and fifty women – and our team of drill instructors had figured out pretty early on that we'd be their "fuck-up division." And, in all honesty, we were fuck-ups. The guidon bearer tripped over a blade of grass and dropped the flag into a dirty creek. Someone absentmindedly adjusted himself in front of our savage lead petty officer, causing her to berate him with nicknames like "Seaman Recruit Little Nuts" and "Dick-Digging Diggler" in front of the entire co-ed company. During marching practice, some kid in the very last rank – his name was "Zelinski" or something weird like that – stepped on the heel of the kid in front of him, setting off a chain reaction of heel-stepping and face-first plummeting.

"Son of a *bitch*, Fatsky!" our chief bellowed at me from across the sea of fallen recruits, using his favorite degrading moniker he'd proudly made up for me. Chief was from Alabama and had a terrifying Southern accent straight out of *Deliverance*, and I was sure he'd make me squeal like a pig at some point before graduation. "Can't you fucking *walk*? I guess I'm gonna have to teach you how to walk!"

And so, we had "walking lessons" for four hours that afternoon: I marched around the entire base of Naval Station Great Lakes with Chief six inches behind me, randomly stomping on my ankles and cackling in delight. When Chief had finally gotten his fill of fun and we returned to the open-bay barracks, the soles of my feet were attached to my flimsy boot camp-issued black socks and my heels were bleeding. Awaiting me on my bunk was my first letter from home, addressed to "Mr. Kevin Zalinsky, Navy Recruit" in the flowy, elegant cursive of the sweetest old lady you can possibly imagine.

Chapter 6:
Separation Anxiety

When I separated from the military, I came home to find there was no *there* there.

"You're moving to Denver? What are you going to do there?"

"Oh, that's cool. What's waiting for you there?"

"Nice! Do you have many friends there?"

"That's exciting! But do you know anybody there?"

"You're not going to be alone there, are you?"

I don't have to set aside an hour every night to iron my uniform and polish my boots. I don't have to wake up at 0530 in the morning. I don't have to be clean-shaven every day or risk being counseled on my professionalism. I don't have to submit daily muster by 0700. I don't even have to keep my ringer turned on, because I don't have duty anymore. There are a lot of things that I don't have to do, but finding the things that I *do* is about as hopeless as an Easter egg hunt in a ball pit.

I can turn my mind off and settle into an unchallenging new routine, or I can attempt to dislodge the ennui with tasks that chip away at the time but ultimately offer no satisfaction. Either way, the state of rest is anything but restful. I have never before been consumed by such a sense of aimlessness; even if I wasn't always entirely sure of my aim, at least I had plenty of distractions to keep me occupied. I found the gnawing *nothing* of my new life to be both dull and excruciating. So, I tried to drown the nothing in alcohol.

"Where have you been?" I was discretely tip-toeing through the kitchen towards the door to the finished basement, where I could hide and sleep away my hangover headache, when my nephew Jacob very loudly called me out. "Whoa! You have *huge bags* under your eyes! Why do you look so bad?"

Jacob was in the living room, sitting cross-legged on the couch, watching PBS on TV and some kind of science experiment tutorial on his tablet. To say the kid is precocious is an understatement; he can probably use "precocious" in a sentence and tell me its etymology. He's whip-smart and has the attitude to back it up. It's a delight to see him wield that sass against my sister or brother-in-law, but it smarts when he turns it on me.

"Shh! Yeah, well, I hung out with some friends last night. I'm just a little tired." I was more than *a little* tired – I bar-hopped until three, lost my date, lost my phone, closed my tab, found my phone, got lost downtown, and slept in my car for four hours.

"You got breakfast for yourself, but you didn't bother to get me anything?" …And then I went to the drive-thru, where I thought only of myself and struggled to pull together enough of my haggard voice to order.

"Uncle Kevin has a hangover. He *needs* this greasy food." That was the hangover commandeering my strained voice; the little grease stains all over the bag were actually rousing a nausea that was making me forget all about the headache.

"Don't teach my eight-year-old kid about hangovers!" my sister yelled from upstairs. I could feel the staircase quake and quiver as she descended; for such a petite person she sure can stomp.

"Uh-oh! I've awakened the beast," I whispered to my nephew as I opened my eyes wide in mock fright. He giggled. I can always make Jacob giggle. I hoped he would remember me fondly after my sister threw me out onto the street.

"There you are! Nice of you to grace us with your presence." Usually when Kelly is irritated, she at least attempts to soften the scorn in her voice with a halfhearted chuckle. Not this time; she was pissed.

"Good morning!" The beast sensed the fear in my voice as I croaked out that phony salutation.

"Jesus, you stumble in at eight in the morning and, Christ on a bike, you look like hell." Kelly grabbed a glass out of the cabinet and filled it with water out of the tap. She thrust it in my direction.

"Coffee, please." Kelly glared at me. If looks could kill, that one would've beaten me to death with the greasy bag of fast food. I took the glass from her, downed it in one very uncomfortable gulp, and let loose an exaggerated *ahhh*. "Never mind, water's good."

"Yeah, I thought so." She took the glass from me and filled it a second time. "You look so dehydrated. I mean, *your face*."

"Okay, I get it. I had a long night, okay?"

"Oh, *you* had a long night? I was worried sick, Kevin. You could have at least called and told me you wouldn't be coming home last night."

"You're right, I should have. I lost my phone, and by the time I found it, the battery was dead. I'm sorry."

"Well, I'm just glad *you're* not dead." The tone of her voice suggested otherwise. No, for as annoyed as she was in that moment, I'm sure my sister would rather I be alive than dead. Still, the alternating pangs of the throbbing headache and the debilitating guilt almost made death seem like a lovely alternative. The women in my family wield guilt like an Irishman wields a set of bagpipes: they stun their foe with an oppressive cacophony that steadily causes disorientation, nausea, shock, and, ultimately, premature death.

"When I agreed to let you live here, I didn't think you'd be pulling this kind of shit."

"Language!" Jacob yelled as he sprang up off the couch. My nephew is like the one-kid Profanity Police. I'm not even allowed to *spell out* a bad word in front of him. If this family were ever stupid enough to use a swear jar, that kid would be loaded and pelting us with onions from the balcony of his mansion as we scurried to take shelter in our cardboard box.

"Sorry, *stuff.*" Kelly poured Jacob a bowl of cereal and placed it on the kitchen counter for him. She turned back to me and continued, in a lowered voice, "This isn't working out."

"What do you mean, 'this isn't working out?' It's not like it's an everyday thing!"

"Yeah, but…" She sighed heavily and smacked her palms down on the countertop. "I can't have you coming into my house half-drunk while my kid's sitting there watching TV. I mean, you *reek.*"

"Well, I sweat off the deodorant." I noisily sniffed my armpit and scrunched up my face; not even a smirk. She really *was* pissed off.

"Don't make jokes. Deodorant doesn't cover up, what, tequila?"

"I don't remember. Look, maybe I went a little overboard. But it's been a long time since I've been able to have fun."

"Don't do that. Don't turn this into me telling you that you're not allowed to have fun. But are you really going to come home from *the Middle East* only to die in Denver, Colorado?"

"Why are you talking about me dying?"

"Because I didn't know where you were! You could've been upside-down in a ditch on the side of the highway!"

"Okay, *Mom.*" Kelly did *not* like that one. If the first look beat me to death with that bag of fast food, this one resurrected me halfway only to shove the entire bag down my throat. "Sorry! Just a joke!"

"That's your problem: you make a joke out of everything. But your nephews won't be laughing when I tell them their Uncle Kevin got drunk and killed downtown."

Ouch. That Irish Catholic Guilt cuts like a hot steak knife through a baked potato.

Kelly stormed out of the kitchen. Phew. "Oh, yeah!" Uh-oh. The beast hadn't yet gotten its fill. "Please don't tell me that you *drove home* from downtown Denver in this condition. Because that would have been *really* stupid. For Christ's sake, my husband is a cop. *Well?*"

I didn't have to answer.

"Of course. *Of course* you drove home like *this*. I hope you realize how lucky you are that you made it back in one piece."

I, again, didn't have to say word. Of course I realized how fortunate I was to have made it home. But I was lucky in more ways than even Kelly, in her all-knowing Taurus superiority, realized. It all started with an unlikely match on Tinder. He seemed like a nice enough guy, if a little curt and sporadic with his messages, and *really* into himself if his shirtless profile pictures were any accurate indication. "We should hang out," read one message sent three days after my last text to him, and two days after I had assumed he just wasn't that into me. I was living with my sister, brother-in-law, and four nephews in the suburbs while I waited to move into my own place in downtown Denver. Living out my Stepford fantasy as a stay-at-home uncle had worn off its novelty. I was *bored*. I couldn't turn down the opportunity to escape suburbia, even if my Tinder match wasn't exactly Mr. Personality. So, I mustered up some enthusiasm and exclamation points and responded, "Sure! Sounds good!"

Now, "hang out" in the modern online parlance has several possible meanings. There's the "hang out" where you watch an episode or two of something on Netflix, subtly inching closer to each other and "accidentally" grazing bodies until you're half-naked and making out while episodes three and four play without interruption and Netflix has to ask if you're still there. There's another "hang out" which is actually a date but neither of you want to call it "a date" for fear of making even the slightest nod towards commitment. "Date" nowadays carries the same weight that I'm assuming "marriage" once did, and that's heavy shit. The final "hang out" is just sex. It's a very literal "hang out" where your genitals hang out with minimal or even zero conversation or name-exchanging beforehand.

"Cool, dude. Let's get Mexican food."

Okay, so "hang out" number three is automatically off the table. We're not going to eat Mexican food and then have anal sex; nobody shall play a game of catch with a gastrointestinal tract full of guacamole, salsa verde, and burritos de machaca. So, it's a date. But that word shall not be used until such a time when the idea of a second not-date is being batted around, at which point one party may coyly ask the other, "Are you asking me out on a date?" which prompts the second party to coyly counter with "Isn't *this* a date?" which then clears the way for the first party to coyly counter-counter with "Oh, is *that* what we're calling this?"

Anyway, we were on our date – sorry, we were *hanging out* – and I quickly realized that the guacamole and I had way more chemistry than me and Mr. Personality. About the only thing we had in common was that we both ordered black beans in our burritos; the stars must have aligned in that moment. He was paying much more attention to his phone than he was to me, but I wasn't at all offended: I can only talk about protein powder and reps and gains so much before I want to unfold my burrito and wrap it around my face until I stop breathing.

I'm having trouble wracking my brain trying to remember every minute detail, but this isn't even about my boring date. It's about what happened a few hours later, when I was alone in downtown Denver, and long after Mr. Personality had ditched me. For the sake of brevity, I had returned to our table from the bathroom to find a note written on a dirty napkin *in crayon* – Mr. P must have borrowed it from one of the kids at the table next to ours – that simply read "Sorry, dude." I felt like I had been dumped by a kindergartener. The kids pointed and giggled, and our waitress brought me a shot of El Toro on the house, but I wasn't at all upset. I have grown to be so jaded by the antics of men that very little surprises me at this stage of my life; I was once broken up with via email on week one of a four-month submarine deployment to the Persian Gulf. At least I got a free shot of tequila out of this deal.

I have come to describe what I encountered later that night as a *darkness*, but not in the sense that I blacked out. My most miserable memories crept out of the recesses of my mind and played over and over in excruciating detail and uncomfortable closeness, just as when I had experienced them in real life. It was all the real pain that I had ever felt – when I watched the light leave Dad's eyes; when Mom broke down on the phone as she told me that MeeMaw was in the hospital and wouldn't be alive by the time I made it home; when I was informed in the middle of the night that my brother had committed suicide on the other side of the world – all that pain was felt anew, all at once in one crippling blow. "*Not this shit again. Why is this happening now? Haven't I dealt with this stuff already? Haven't I moved on? Give me a fucking break.*" Is it always here, I wonder, lurking just beneath the surface and lured out with a few shots of Fireball and some gnarly concoction called "Devil's Brew?" The pain seeped out of my every pore, it crushed my throat, it strangled my heart, it stabbed me in the gut, it *hurt*. And there I was: drunk, alone, hurting, and stumbling down unknown streets with a dead phone battery.

I leaned up against a cement wall, outside some dive bar where the lingering remnants of the last-call crowd were adding new contacts to their phones before dispersing. I was at least mindful enough not to stand in the puddle of puke on the sidewalk. My eyes were burning, my cheeks were stinging, and I had no idea how I was going to pull enough of myself together to find my car so I could crash. Not in the literal sense; I needed to *sleep*. I was so exhausted, I considered sleeping right then and there, propped up against that wall. I felt my car keys in my pocket; I hadn't even noticed that they were digging into my thigh. That pain was so insignificant in comparison. That's when I met Carson.

"Wow, man. You look like shit." He was dressed in all black, like an angel of the night out of some hokey country music ballad.

"Thanks, Johnny Cash." I was proud of myself; even in that pitiful state I managed to pull an appropriate dis out of my drunken ass.

"What's going on? Come on, man, you're standing in barf." He was right; I must have teetered into the puddle while trying to think of who he reminded me of. He put his hand on my shoulder and steered me out of the puke and onto a clean patch of sidewalk.

"Thanks," I'm sure I spit in a most ungrateful tone as I leaned back against the wall.

"So, you wanna talk about it? It looks like you've been through it tonight."

"Yeah, I look like shit, remember?"

"Sorry about that, man. It's just that I saw you earlier at Neon Triangle and you looked, uh...*different* than you do right now. I wasn't even sure if you were the same guy."

"*He was at Neon Triangle?*" Neon Triangle is the kind of gay club that's designed to actively repel straight men, or at least those straight men who are so delusional in their self-appraisal that they assume gay men won't be able to control their dangerous gay urges around them: boy-on-boy twerking, twinks in little go-go shorts serving shots called "blow jobs," late-2000s Madonna songs. Johnny Cash didn't exactly look like the kind of guy who I'd expect to frequent a place like Neon Triangle, although he was certainly a looker upon closer inspection.

"*You* were at Neon Triangle?" God, I hope I didn't bat my eyelashes or attempt to make some kind of sexy face in that unruly state.

"Yeah, I was there," he chuckled. I must have made a sexy face. Damn it. "Come on, let me get you into a taxi."

"No, that would be way too expensive." I pulled my car keys out of my pocket and jangled them in the air. "I'm staying in...uh...*somewhere* in suburbia right now."

"Uh, no. You're not driving like this." Johnny Cash made a grab at my keys but I snatched them away with a surprising quickness.

"My car is...also *somewhere*." I wildly gestured with both arms in no specific direction. "I'm gonna sleep in my car."

"In *this* neighborhood? Oh boy." If a man dressed in all black with a tattoo on his neck looks around and says "oh boy," you know the neighborhood can't be great.

"No, I don't think it's close. It's on a street like Alvada, or Arvava, or Avdada, or...I don't know."

"You mean Arvada? That's like eight blocks over, man. If you insist on sleeping in your car, I'm gonna have to insist on walking with you."

How could I refuse? I was trashed, I was exhausted, I was lost, I didn't have a usable phone which meant I didn't have Google Maps, and my judgment was about as impaired as the rest of my bodily processes, so I didn't bother putting up a fight. "Fine. Just don't kill me, please."

"Ha. Deal! Name's Carson, by the way." So, Johnny Cash turned out to be Johnny Carson; I never did reveal my little mnemonic trick for remembering his name. "And you are?"

"Kevin," and very surprised that I could remember my own name at that point. "Thanks, Carson."

"No problem, Kevin. So, where are you from? What's your deal?"

As we walked, or, in my case, tottered like a giant baby who'd had one too many bottles of formula, I told him my deal. I just got out of the Navy after eleven years and moved from Bahrain to Denver. My sister and her family are here, but otherwise I don't know anybody. They live in the suburbs and I can't wait to move into my own place. I had a boring Tinder date that lead nowhere except to my being drunk and lost in a strange city. I also shoehorned in excruciating details about Dad, MeeMaw, and Kyle, just to sweeten the pot. I felt sorry for myself as I told this harrowing tale of loss and sadness, but I felt even worse for Carson. Surely he hadn't anticipated *this* being a part of his evening's itinerary? As I blathered away, I'd occasionally veer just a little too close to the street and Carson would grab me by the shoulders and set me back on course; I'm grateful he didn't just let me walk into traffic to put us both out of our misery.

"Wow, man. Damn." Carson shook his head in disbelief. "You've been through some shit, huh? But...if you don't mind me making a little observation?"

I responded with a resigned shrug of the shoulders. The odds were razor-thin that this near stranger could say anything that would sink me further into the muck that had become my Friday night.

"It sounds like you haven't really dealt with things," Carson warily suggested, gauging my reaction before continuing, "And it sounds like booze is *not* your friend."

"Tell me about it." It had become painfully obvious, even to my currently hammered, ever delusional self, that alcohol has never been, nor will ever be, a dependable ally or trustworthy bosom buddy. I tell myself ridiculous things like "it'll be different *this time*" or "it won't have a negative effect on me *this time*" or "I'll hold my liquor much better *this time*." But when, if "this time" becomes "every time" without fail, does enough become *enough*?

"Sorry, Kevin. You have *way more* than enough on your plate right now. I didn't mean to pile on more shit. Just...maybe think about it in the morning?"

"I will, I will." I did. Maybe it was the astute observations of a stranger, maybe it was my frustrations with a perpetual cycle that I never seem willing or able to break, or maybe it was my sister's masterful command of Irish Catholic Guilt, but *something* prompted me to, as Carson urged, "think about it."

"There it is!" Eventually we found my car. Rather, Carson found my car based off of the incoherent description I had given him; the fact that it had a Georgia license plate probably helped him pick it out of the bunch. Thankfully, it hadn't been towed from the spot where I had parked it the evening before. No parking tickets, either! What a sorry state of affairs it is when the lack of a parking ticket is the highlight of your weekend night out on the town.

"Are you *sure* you want to sleep in your car? I have a couch."

"No, I'll be fine." Even if I *was* seven sheets to the wind, I wasn't so far gone that I couldn't feel the dual sting of shame and humiliation. "I promise I'll be fine."

"Alright, Kevin. I'd put my number in your phone, but…well, you know. May I have your number?"

I didn't hesitate to give Carson my phone number, although I'm sure I tried and failed to act coy. As it turns out, I gave him the wrong phone number. Reading my account of this evening's events, I imagine one might think, "Yeah, right. You're such a mess. This guy was obviously just trying to be nice to you. You gave him the right number; he just didn't save it. He was probably pretending to type. Face it: you're a loser!" to which I'd respond, "I get it! You made your point. Give me a fucking break." I'd meet Carson again a few weeks later – thanks to Tinder, no less – and he'd show me that he did, indeed, save me to his contacts list, but the number I had given him in that state of inebriation was all jumbled up and contained digits that aren't even part of my actual phone number.

So, after unintentionally giving him a fake phone number, Carson unlocked the passenger door, helped me plop down into the seat, and dropped the keys in the center console. The last thing I remember, as my heavy eyelids came crashing down, is him leaning down and kissing me on the forehead before softly closing the car door. It sounds so romantic, but I tracked vomit into my car so it smelled like the men's bathroom at the Port Authority on a mid-July afternoon by the time I woke up.

Chapter 7:
My First Time

I never once had sex before I joined the Navy. I was a virgin for twenty-one years, and, for a good quarter of those years, I had these dreamy, romantic, nebulous, unrealistic ideas of how my first sexual experience would go. My virginity would be taken gently from me as would any precious thing, and my one true love would treasure and revere me for having gifted it unto him. Of course, reality never mirrors our fantasies.

I woke up that morning with a savage migraine. My tongue was stuck to the roof of my mouth; they had fused together into one dry mass that crackled like pork rinds when pulled apart. My neck was so stiff, I could barely lift my head up off the pillow. Turning to look at the alarm clock was a great struggle; it was past ten. I am never capable of sleeping past six thirty, especially when I'm still half-drunk from the night before. I noticed that the curtains in my barracks room had been pulled shut, but I never sleep in complete darkness because I'm still afraid of what might be lurking in the shadows. It suddenly made perfect sense why I hadn't woken up at my usual time: the Hawaiian sun couldn't flick my eyelids with an annoyingly chipper "Aloha!"

The rest of my body was about as stiff as my neck, but I began to notice the discomfort as I stirred. My arms felt like they had been twisted backwards and released just before the snapping point; they laid limp at my sides. My legs, too, were like slabs of dense, lifeless flesh. My toes hurt as if they had all been stubbed at once, and were curled up to keep from becoming detached and falling off my feet. My fingers, tingling as they woke, were next to draw my attention to their pain. "*Was I clawing at concrete? Why do my fingernails feel like they could be peeled clean off?*" I couldn't muster the energy to draw my hands from beneath the covers to look at them, but I could feel something sticky on the tips of my nails and in between my fingers. By that point I could smell the blood.

My room smelled like coins, like piles of a dozen peoples' spare change. No, not my room – my bed. *"Did I get in a fight last night? I must have lost – it feels like I got the shit kicked out of me. Did I get in trouble again? How did I get into my bed? How– no, why did I take all my clothes off?"* I never sleep naked; I'm too self-conscious to share a bed with *myself* if I'm not fully clothed. I winced as I attempted to hoist my body: first my head, followed by my limbs, all at once and then individually in no particular order, and finally my core. When I tried to lift my torso, I felt the pain course through my entire body like I was on a serrated skewer.

With a guttural groan, I flung myself onto my left side; at that point I could no longer ignore the great ache in my midsection. It was a sharp pain, much different from the dull soreness the rest of my body had sunken into. I ran my right hand over my belly, expecting to feel scrapes, cuts, wounds, dried blood – anything indicative of a brutal brawl. I realized then that my injuries were internal. My gut felt heavy and rotted, like a malignant tumor had invaded my abdominal cavity and was now festering in its own muck. But no, not my stomach. This pain was somewhere else, lower and deeper in a place I hadn't before noticed, not once.

I grabbed the flimsy bedside table and dragged myself to the edge of the bed; my fingernails felt like they might crack and pop off under the strain. I thrust myself into the upright seated position with my left elbow, not giving it too much thought lest I lose the nerve for such a bold exertion. When my feet swung off the bed and hit the floor, I heard the clatter of empty plastic Solo cups. I swept them aside with my foot and felt something entirely different when I returned it to the grungy carpet: a slimy, sticky, squishy piece of rubber. I recoiled both feet in disgust and peered over the tops of my knees at the floor beneath me. I had never seen one in real life, much less felt one after it had been used for its intended purpose, but I knew instantly what I had just stepped on.

I sprang out of bed. Putting the entirety of my 220 pounds on my feet caused the pain to rip through my insides. I doubled over and grabbed onto my rumpled bedsheet in desperation; I thought I'd rip it clear off the bed. It was then, when I was hunched over and gripping that threadbare sheet to keep from falling backwards, that I saw the blood. Most of it had dried, but some was pooling in the center of the mattress where my butt had formed an indention over the months. I don't know exactly how much there was; my eyes immediately darted away, looking instead at the grimy barracks wall. My mind shut off. I felt my breathing become quick and shallow; I felt my back become tense and the hairs on my neck stand up; I felt my forehead throbbing with the migraine that had since become gargantuan yet remained the very least of my concerns; I felt the scratchy sheets in my trembling hands; I felt the squishy rubber with the big toe of my right foot; and I felt the pain in my midsection becoming fainter as gravity pulled it downwards. But I didn't think. I wasn't capable of thinking. My mind was vacant.

I didn't scream, or cry, or lose my balance, or faint, or break my fist against the wall, or react with any emotion whatsoever. I understood, in the space of a second, exactly how that blood had come to be pooling in the middle of my bed. I became aware, suddenly and unmistakably, of the blood caked on the backs and insides of my thighs. I released the bedsheet from my death grip and stood as erect as possible. I trudged from my bed to the dingy little bathroom, displacing more Solo cups as I moved. All the while, I stared straight ahead, through whichever object happened to be in my line of sight, never allowing my eyes to focus.

When I reached the bathroom, I didn't turn on the overhead fluorescent light and I certainly didn't look in the mirror. I reached into the shower and turned on the water – first the cold, all the way, and then the hot, just a tiny bit. I felt the water with the back of my hand and held it there for a few long minutes, making unmistakably sure it didn't get too warm. I allowed my gaze to join me in the bathroom only when it came time to step into the shower. I squeezed my eyes tight as the water hit my face and then my chest before streaming down the front of my body. Once my mind exited self-preservation mode and allowed itself to power back on, I realized that I had again doubled over, this time clutching my knees for support. I was frozen; I was terrified of what I would feel if I turned around, of what I would see if I looked down at the water as it circled the drain.

After what must have been a half hour, I very slowly and very reluctantly turned to face the wall of the shower, grasping at the tiles and digging into the grout with my sore fingers. I looked up at the chipped bathroom ceiling; I refused to look anywhere else. When the water hit my backside, I felt an unbearable sting that I can – and often do – recall to this day. It felt like the water was actually tiny shards of glass, slicing into that most sensitive area and opening up hundreds of microscopic wounds which cried out in unified agony. It was a searing pain that I can't believe didn't bring me to my knees and leave me crumpled and prostrate on the shower floor.

I cried for the first time since making that horrifying discovery. I sobbed so hard that my entire body heaved; I sobbed so hard that my forehead banged against the tiled shower wall. I felt alone, so absolutely and unnervingly alone. The pristine beaches of Oahu – and their happy, shiny, beautiful tourists – must have been swallowed up by the angry sea, tossed like crumbs into its giant maw. My pain surely reverberated throughout the universe, felt by anything and everything with a pulse; anyone who survived certainly wouldn't be left smiling. Life couldn't have marched on unobstructed, without missing a beat, without stumbling or pausing as my cries rang out like the pealing of a funeral bell.

And yet, of course life went on. In two short days I'd be on a plane, heading to Japan for my very first deployment. I quite literally didn't have time to deal with what I had woken up to on that Saturday morning. So, I pushed it down: deep inside with the awful pain which lingered for days before fading into an aching numbness. I'd learned how to work through the pain, how to maneuver through my days with that persistent ache. Every so often I'd feel a twinge and panic: *"Am I making it worse? Did something just rip? Am I bleeding again?"* I'd duck into a bathroom stall, pull the top half of my coveralls down and let them drop to the floor, and, as discretely as possible, check for blood. Most times, there was a little bit; I'd look at it, there on my fingertips, and my eyes would sting. But I couldn't, as much as I might have been compelled to, drop to my knees and break down in tears. "Yo, let's go, Zalinsky!"

"Petty Officer Zalinsky…? Mr. Zalinsky?"

"Oh, um…Yeah?"

Thankfully, I wasn't currently hiding in a grimy bathroom stall and checking for blood, although my body recalled the pain I felt as if it had happened just that morning. I was in a custodian's closet in Frankfurt that had been turned into a makeshift Veteran's Affairs office. The VA representative, Miss Karen, sat on an overturned crate and used a wobbly-legged table the janitor had pulled out from underneath some disused staircase. She'd furiously take notes – trying her best to move expeditiously through the line of service members which stretched down the hospital corridor, doubled back on itself, and only seemed to grow with each person processed – and the table would shimmy and knock into a crusty mop that was propped up against the wall. "I'm sorry, ma'am, what was your question?"

"Is there any other trauma you'd like to discuss while you have me here in front of you? Because, as it stands, we can't consider your depression over the deaths of your father and brother service-related, and therefore, with all likelihood, you won't receive any compensation for psychological distress."

"Oh. Even though my work was affected?"

"Well, yes, even if your work suffered a bit because of it. The VA looks at that sort of trauma as…well, normal, and not something specifically exacerbated by your employment. Now, if there were proof that you had ongoing issues and had sought additional treatment over the years, that would be a different story, but…we've established that you haven't talked to any psychiatrists or therapists prior to today." Miss Karen ripped through her talking points with lightning speed, as if she had given a similar spiel once or twice within the past ten minutes, and also in an adorable Southern accent which made me yearn for America even more.

"Oh. Okay." I attribute my utter lack of enthusiasm over just how disabled the Navy has made me to a few things: a. I had such low expectations regarding the VA that I was impressed that Miss Karen had the right person's file in front of her when I'd knocked and entered the closet; b. I had started to seriously reconsider my intentions of separating from the military and effectively restarting my life; c. thinking of that dreadful Saturday morning in February 2009 has a tendency to paralyze my body and disable my mind; and d. I was in a fucking janitor's closet. But I tried not to hold anything against Miss Karen; I got the impression that she was really trying her best given the circumstances.

"Now, back to my question: did you experience anything *during the period of your active duty service* that you'd like to claim? Anything that might have resulted in something like anxiety or PTSD?"

"Um…no. No, there's nothing."

"Are you sure? Think, now. A lot can happen in eleven years, Mr. Zalinsky." Bless her, she really was trying to throw me a bone. But I hadn't discussed those events with anybody – not Mom, not Kelly, not Kyle, not anybody – in nine years, and I couldn't imagine myself kicking things off in a closet that smelled like Pine-Sol and mildew. "Remember, there's no statute of limitations on reporting something."

"Yeah, I'm sure, ma'am. There's nothing." A coworker told me, about a month before my separation interview, that he had been hooked up to a polygraph machine during his own interview. Thankfully, he was full of shit; that poor machine would've been smoking and sputtering after that series of answers.

"Okay, then! Well, before we say goodbye, I *did* notice that you were referred for alcohol dependency in…Hawaii! Oh, Hawaii's just beautiful. Anyway, do you ever drink nowadays?"

"No, not at all." The imaginary machine exploded after that whopper.

"I'm glad to hear it. I sincerely hope that you maintain your abstinence, and also that your new civilian life brings you nothing but success and happiness."

"Oh, thank you so m—"

"Next!" Miss Karen slammed my file shut and tossed it into a cardboard box under her wobbly table. The next guy in line squeezed past me into the closet; I heard the frame of the doorway splinter and groan. He exhaled in my face and I could smell the lovely pairing of wintergreen chew and Monster on his hot breath. That brought me right back to the halcyon days of one gung-ho, baby-faced Seaman Apprentice Zalinsky, slamming twenty-four-ounce energy drinks and bumming pouches of chewing tobacco in the smoke pit, all in a sad and fruitless grab at coolness. I'm glad I gave that shit up; there's nothing "cool" about being able to truthfully claim mouth or lung cancer on one's disability compensation request form.

In the hallway, everyone had leaned up against the wall and was either playing on their phone or counting the cracks in the ceiling tiles. "Good luck," I said, mostly to myself.

The first thing I did upon returning to my hotel room was pour myself a glass of bourbon. Normally I'd cut it down with a splash of Coke, but I skipped the pretense this time. I downed the glass in a few gulps, kicked my shoes off, and climbed into bed. I was a little hungry, but I'd eaten enough doner kebab in those four days to last me at least three lifetimes. Instead, I watched the fluffy snow drift gently past the window as the sunlight faded; it was only four thirty in the afternoon.

One thing I was certain I'd miss about the Middle East is the sun, especially at sunrise: that giant, hazy red orb that sets the flight line ablaze as if it were on Tatooine. Germany doesn't have a sun like that, but neither does Denver. The snow reminded me that a new life was awaiting me: a life of seasons, occasional cold, dispensaries on every corner, and freedom. I was confident that I'd be ready for such drastic change; I was positive that my anxiety, my sadness, my heartbreak – these were all things of the past. There would be no room for them in my new life. That was my last night in Germany before I returned to Bahrain, where I'd finish out my last few months of active duty service before skipping gaily into that new life.

Chapter 8:
Beast

As was previously mentioned, my sister is tiny. But she makes up for her diminutive stature with *ferocity*. She's a beast trapped in the body of a pixie. I was probably twelve at the time, so Satan was fifteen and Beast was twenty-two. She was home on leave from the Navy. At the time she was stationed in Meridian, Mississippi, and she hadn't been home since before boot camp two years prior. She had bearing, she had presence, she had manners, she had a non-faddish shoulder-length bob haircut. It was a little dorky, but I was afraid if I made fun of her she'd make me drop and give her twenty. This wasn't the same Kelly who'd worn acid-washed denim and sang *Like a Virgin* into a hairbrush. I was so excited that my cool big sister was home for an entire week, especially so when she came to my rescue and *beat the shit out of Kyle*.

It was the Friday evening before the Monday Kelly was to report back to her command. Mom called to let her know she'd be going grocery shopping after work, and asked that she please Frankenstein dinner together for her brothers to make room in the fridge for new food. Now, Kelly had not joined the Navy to be a culinary specialist, and it showed. I have never been, by any stretch of the imagination, a picky eater – as a baby I'd crawl into the cabinet under the kitchen sink and chomp on dog biscuits – but her concoction gave even me pause. I remember some kind of meat mixed with some kind of...I wanna say beans? then topped off with some kind of chunky sauce. I expected this thing to growl at me if I came too close with a fork. The reason I so clearly remember this gastronomical nightmare is because, upon taking my first apprehensive bite, Kyle smacked me on the back of the head and I started to choke.

Now, I was an excitable fatty in my youth, so I was no stranger to choking on food prior to this particular incident. Once, when I was seven, I ran out of MeeMaw's house to greet Mom when she came to pick me up. Running and hard candy don't mix, especially when the "running" in question is really a foot-dragging shuffle complicated by heavy asthmatic breathing. Luckily, Mom dislodged that hard candy from my obese throat with ease, and I lived to shove my sausage fingers into the bowl of candy MeeMaw had on a table next to her front door. On this particular evening, however, I was not fortunate enough to choke on the caramel decadence that is a Werther's Original hard candy. I instead choked on the culinary calamity of one Seaman Recruit Kelly Zalinsky. It was saltier than the tears pooling in my eyes; the cries of my lungs, begging for air, were drowned out by my taste buds' screams for mercy.

Kyle bolted out of the dining room, through the kitchen, and up the stairs. Kelly shoved her chair out from underneath the table and sprang after him with lightning speed. "Don't you *ever* hit your brother on the back of his head while he's eating!" she screamed after him as he took the stairs two by two, cackling like a delighted devil. Meanwhile, I was still choking, but I managed to cough the wriggling piece of gray *whatever it was* free and onto the table. I scrambled after Kelly, cheering her on with hoarse cries of "Get him!" What I saw when I made it up the stairs was sweeter than the very life I had snatched from the jaws of that salty abomination we called "dinner."

Kyle was taunting Kelly from down the hallway, standing with his hand on the knob of his bedroom door and ready to slam it in her face if she made an attempt to charge. Instead, Kelly made small, virtually undetectable movements that I noticed only because I was standing a foot behind her at the top of the stairs. "Good, you stopped choking," she said to me under her breath. While Kyle heckled and writhed in self-satisfied glee, Kelly moved her right leg backward, ever so subtly, and pivoted her weight onto the ball of her left foot. She then *sprang* off the hardwood floor and literally *flew* through the air. By the time he realized what was happening, Kelly was plummeting into Kyle and hauling him down onto the floor with all 115 pounds of her rage. Luckily for Kyle, our bedrooms at 1280 Glenn Avenue had carpeting, so his fall was cushioned. However, his fortune was short-lived.

Kelly grabbed him by the hair and started slamming his head against the floor. Kyle elbowed her in the face. Blood sprayed out of Kelly's nose and onto the carpet, the back of Kyle's head, and all over her hands which had maintained their death grip on his hair. From my angle, it looked like Kelly was clawing Kyle's head into a bloody pulp. It was a good thing I hadn't swallowed that gray matter – I would've hurled. She grabbed his head like a CrossFitter might grip a rubber slam ball, pulled it back as far as she could, and *bashed* his face into the carpet with furious finality.

And his braces got stuck in the carpet. Kelly jumped up as Kyle's limbs started to violently slap around like loose garden hoses. It was like watching a great mountain lion that had gotten its paw caught in a trap: wounded and frightened, but still very much alive and *pissed off.* His muffled screams shook the whole floor of his bedroom with a bone-chilling rage.

"Should we just leave him here until he breaks free?" Kelly asked, just as panicked and frozen in her tracks as I was. This elicited a great bellow from our captive cat. "Calm down! It's your own damn fault that you're in this position!"

"Great, Kelly. Antagonize Kyle two days before you return to the safety of anywhere but here and leave me to suffer the consequences. He'll beat the shit out of me!"

"What the *hell* is going on up there?" Mom screamed upstairs from the kitchen. I could hear the rustling of paper grocery bags. "Don't worry about helping me bring in the groceries! I do everything else in this goddamn house, so I might as well bring in twenty bags of food by myself, too." After a pause: "And what the *hell* is this on the table? Please don't tell me *this* is what you made for dinner?"

"Mom, we're kinda in the middle of something up here!" Kelly yelled down, remaining clear of Kyle's flailing limbs. Both she and I had assumed the fleeing stance just in case those precious carpet fibers should snap and set him loose.

"Oh, for Christ's sake." We heard Mom's heavy footfall on the stairs. She, like Kelly, sure could stomp up and down the stairs for someone so petite. "Jesus Christ!" Mom exclaimed when she came into Kyle's bedroom and saw two of her kids, one of whom had bloodied hands, standing over her third kid, who had blood-matted hair. "There's blood all over the carpet!"

"His braces are stuck," Kelly sheepishly explained to Mom. Even Kelly, Queen Becky of Sass-upon-Attitude, realized that this particular moment called for a less flippant approach than her usual.

"Are you kidding me?" Mom threw her hands up in exasperation. "Do you have any idea how expensive braces are? Kyle, are you okay?"

Kyle gave the screaming and thrashing a rest when Mom came over to investigate. She moved his long hair out of his face to get a better look at this fusion of metal and shag, and saw that both rows of teeth were entangled. He whimpered pitifully as a grab for even more sympathy than this humiliating position had already gifted him. "Oh, my God. We're gonna have to cut you loose!"

"He started it, Mom!" Kelly was having none of this pathetic display of false victimhood. "He hit Kevin on the back of the head while he was eating!"

"What *is* that that you made, anyway?" Mom apparently couldn't get over that squirming mass of brown and gray. She scrunched up her face in disgust. I'm sure if I *had* choked to death, she would be less concerned with Frankendinner.

"Some leftover meat I found in the back of the fridge, a can of beans, half jars of gravy, spaghetti sauce, and...oh yeah, mango salsa, all mixed together." Mom and I both stared at her in disbelief. I'm sure Kyle would have, too, were his face not presently attached to the carpet. "What? You *told me* to use up old food to make room for new stuff!"

"What's going on up here?" Dad had gotten home from work and came upstairs to join us. He still had his work shirt and shoes on, and his car keys and wallet were in his hands. His reaction was less aggravated than Mom's, per usual: he shook his head and chuckled when he saw what his darling family had gotten up to. "Is Kyle okay?"

"His braces are stuck to the carpet!" I all-too-gleefully informed him.

He raised his eyebrows in mock shock, but I'm sure nothing actually surprised Dad when it came to his kids. He chuckled again and said "I'll go get the scissors" as he turned and went back down the hallway.

"Kelly, go clean up your face and hands. That's disgusting." Mom took Kelly by the shoulders and led her out of the room and into the hallway. "Kevin, let's go throw away your sister's 'dinner' and order pizza. And we still have to put the groceries away."

Kyle flopped pathetically like a fish on the dock and whimpered, just in case we had forgotten about him. Truthfully, I *had* forgotten about him since he was physically restrained and practically mute. Those few minutes of relative peace and quiet with Mom, Dad, and Kelly were quite pleasant! Except for the blood all over my sister's face and hands, of course. "Oh, don't worry, Honey." I think Mom might have forgotten about him, too. "Dad will be up with scissors to cut you loose. But *don't* come picking a fight with your brother or sister when you're free!"

Mom and I left the room, and I'm sure I had a smugly satisfied look on my face. I had, after all, survived choking on briny mystery meat and lived to see Kyle in such a compromising position as this. I never thought I'd see him on the receiving end of a beatdown, nor could I have imagined that Kelly would rush to my defense in such a glorious display of savagery. Still, I dared not taunt him as we left him there; I was far too fat and bottom-heavy to make myself airborne and fly down the hallway like Crouching Kelly, Hidden Sister. He may have been momentarily weakened, but, like a demon wounded during an exorcism, it would only be a matter of time before he was back on his hooves and terrorizing the innocent.

Mom and I passed Dad, scissors in hand, in the hallway. He patted me on the head with his free hand and looked at me as if to say, "Don't be too close when he's free from the trap." And so Dad cut his eldest son free from the carpet, and Kyle trudged down the hall to the bathroom to nurse his wounds and pick the fibrous remnants from his braces. By the time he joined the rest of us downstairs in the kitchen, the pizza had been delivered. Sulky and defeated, he ate in silence.

Chapter 9:
The Airport Incident

Mom and Kelly haven't always had the most harmonious relationship. But when the two of them begrudgingly remove their swords from each other's throats and join forces in a temporary alliance, their combined power is a force to be reckoned with. I shall now regale you with a tale – one such example of this unified might – which has since come to be known as "the Airport Incident." While I was not present for the events comprising this tale, I can see every minute detail so vividly, recall every single word as if it were uttered directly into my ear.

Surely I must be misremembering? How else, if I hadn't experienced these events firsthand, can it all be so clear to me? Oh, right: because Mom tells this damn story every single time more than five people in our family gather in one place. This tale has woven itself into the storied fabric of our genealogy through sheer force of repetition. If our family's history were ever gathered into a single tome, it would handily match the Bible – in volume, if not quality, although some of those stories are questionable – and this one would be our version of *David and Goliath*. Ladies and gentlemen, for your entertainment: the Airport Incident, aka *Kathy and Goliath*.

Mom took Kelly's best friend, Sarah, and drove from Union to Newark Liberty International Airport to pick up Kelly. She had just been discharged from the Navy and was visiting New Jersey before resuming her civilian life in Portland, Oregon. Kelly was seven months pregnant with her first son, Matthew, at the time. I'm not sure if airlines had restrictions regarding pregnant passengers in those days. Was this before doctors started advising expecting mothers to not drink or smoke? I think Jimmy Carter was president at the time. Okay, okay, no more "old" jokes. As has already been illustrated, Beast can throw down. And, for the record, it was Bill Clinton.

As she pulled up to the airport, Mom staked out the perfect spot at curbside passenger pick-up: right in front of the door. All Kelly had to was waddle her pregnant ass through the door and plop down into the front seat of the station wagon, and they'd be off. Unfortunately, as Mom describes him, "some fat fucking slob" had plans of his own, plans that were at direct odds with hers. This is like telling somebody the events of World War II and trying to maintain some kind of suspense as to who wins the thing. This rotund, slovenly fellow had no chance of surviving this storm; remember, she was still Hurricane Kathy back then.

"Son of a *bitch*!" Mom yelled as her chunky nemesis cut in front of her from two lanes over and *stole her parking spot*. "Oh no. Not *today*." Mom laid on her horn with one hand and gestured wildly with the other.

Kelly's friend Sarah was a nervous, perpetually shaking girl. "Um…Mrs. Zalinsky? Maybe we can find another spot? I'm sure there are some jus—"

"Oh no! That fat son of a bitch saw me!" As she spoke, Mom maintained eye contact with the spot-stealer in his rearview mirror. She whipped her head to glare at Sarah, probably prompting the poor girl to soil herself. "*I had my blinker on.*"

If ever one could make "I had my blinker on" a viable defense for any given infraction – road rage, intentional collision, vehicular homicide – Mom could. Nobody will *ever* be able to look Mom in the face as she tells this story and say, "You had your blinker on? So what? That doesn't matter." Mom is so unyielding in her innocence, so unwavering about the indisputable defense afforded by the use of the blinker, so pure and noble a thing. "I had my blinker on! That fat bastard probably saw us – a middle-aged lady and a shaky little girl – and thought 'Hur hur, that spot's mine! Those broads ain't gonna do nothing!' and he stole my spot! So I beeped my horn!"

Mom didn't just toot her horn, I'm sure of it. I can easily imagine her laying all her weight on the steering wheel and digging both palms into that horn. As Mom furiously honked and Sarah sank lower into her seat, Kelly emerged from baggage claim just in time for "A Very Zalinsky Family Reunion." The spot-stealer flung his door open and rolled out of his car, scattering candy wrappers and empty potato chip bags all over the road, as Mom tells it. He trudged his way to her car, screaming and flailing his arms as he went, and apparently shoved some little old man who was unfortunate enough to cross paths with this decimator of social norms. Mom, being the gallant warrior of justice, rightness, and blinkers that she is, couldn't just sit back and honk the horn as these egregious acts unfolded. So, she got out of her car.

"Um, Mrs. Zalinsky, maybe you should stay in the car?" Sarah meekly and futilely suggested. "L-look! K-Kelly's here! Shouldn't we get her and lea—"

"Stay in the car, Sarah!" Mom slammed the car door behind her. She crossed her arms and leaned up against the side of the station wagon, baiting her incensed enemy. "You have *some* nerve!"

"Mom, hi…What's going on here?" Kelly had made her way to the car at last, leaving her luggage on the sidewalk before waddling over to Mom's side. Sarah, meanwhile, was peeking over the top of the dashboard.

"What's your problem?" the spot-stealer snarled at an unflinching Mom. He was a great, sweaty, sloppy man, his button-up shirt half-tucked into his loose-fitting, food-stained sweatpants. His yellowed undershirt rode up just enough to reveal a gargantuan, hairy belly.

"You stole my spot! *I had my blinker on*, and you swooped right in front of me to steal it!"

"Mom, is this really—"

"So what? It's my spot now! Get over it, bitch!" If this slimy behemoth had earned even a sliver of understanding from Kelly, in that second it disappeared quicker than a fistful of Cheetos in his chubby paw.

"Don't talk to my mother that way." Kelly lowered her voice and clenched her jaw. She squared up against the man as if she *didn't* have swollen ankles and a protruding belly that could rival even his. "Get back in your car and leave us alone."

"And what are *you* gonna do if I don't, you pregnant bitch?"

Game on. Mom flung herself at the beast like a cat after a toy mouse. She struck his fat cheeks while wailing "Don't you *dare* talk to my daughter that way!" He slammed Mom against the hood of the station wagon and raised a great fist. Mom rolled out of the way just in time to watch that mallet come crashing down, leaving a huge crater upon impact. She may have been momentarily stunned, but she snapped out of it when he roared and stomped the ground like an irate yeti. Poor Sarah was on the floor in the fetal position by this point.

Mom grabbed him by the collar of his stained shirt while Kelly, pregnant belly and all, leapt onto his back and wrapped both arms around his giant neck. He flailed about in an attempt to shake Kelly loose, but she grabbed his nose with one hand and ground the knuckles of the other into his eyes, as if fighting off an enormous great white. Mom was pulling on his collar with such force that the buttons of his shirt started ricocheting off and hitting the windshield.

"His buttons started popping off!" Mom loves this part of the story, and always delights in pointing at the imaginary buttons as they fly past her head. "Ping...ping...ping!"

Eventually, despite his best efforts to flip her over his head and onto the pavement, Kelly succeeding in bringing the beast to his knees by kicking the backs of his legs. She released his head from her suffocating embrace and jumped down onto the sidewalk. Mom let go of his collar and he slumped onto his belly in defeat. "You crazy bitches!"

"Think twice before you steal another spot, you asshole!" Mom kicked at the ground in front of him, sending dirt and buttons flying into his face. "Kelly, let's go!"

Sarah emerged from her hiding spot only after peeking out from behind the car door to see if the dust had settled. She grabbed Kelly's luggage and threw it, along with herself, into the backseat. Mom and Kelly leaned over their vanquished foe to hug hello, Mom put her hand on Kelly's belly as if to say "You're okay in there," and the two of them jumped in the station wagon. Mom pulled away from the scene of the scuffle and drove off, resisting the urge to run over her nemesis; he had since managed to bring himself to his hands and knees. Some people might be shocked to learn that no cops or good Samaritans felt compelled to break up a fight between a humongous man and two women, one of whom was unmistakably pregnant, or even investigate once it was over and a person was lying in the middle of the street. But those people obviously aren't from New Jersey.

"Hi, Kelly," Sarah squeaked from the backseat, where she was lying down from the overwhelming exhaustion.

"Hi, Sarah! How have you been?" Kelly proceeded to fix her bangs in the mirror of the passenger-side visor. "It's good to finally be on the ground! That flight was long."

"Did you have a good seat, Sweetie?" Mom reached over to straighten Kelly's collar which had *somehow* gotten ruffled and flipped up. "This is a cute blouse."

"Thanks! And yeah, I had an aisle seat, so I was able to stretch my legs a little bit." Kelly flipped the visor up and turned halfway to look at Mom. "Hey, I'm starving!"

"Me too! Wanna stop at Luigi's on the way home?"

"How can you two *eat* at a time like this?" Sarah asked incredulously, as if it were so inconceivable that one would work up a little appetite during a street brawl.

We fight in this family. Most of the time we fight amongst ourselves, sometimes we fight complete strangers, but we fight. Mom has always said "It's the principle of the thing." She said that just last week, actually; she got in hot water with the homeowners' association at her retired living community because she left a "colorful" – translated from Momspeak to "profanity-ridden" – note on the front door of a neighbor who didn't clean up the nuggets left by his dog on her front lawn. She picked a fight by leaving that note, F-bombs and all, for "the principle of the thing."

What principle, what thing – they're usually nebulous and not very easily defined, but that's beside the point. We fight for what we know is right – getting a spot close to the door so a very pregnant Kelly doesn't have to walk too far, or, let's be honest, getting that spot because Mom was there first and therefore entitled to it – and we move on once we've made our point. Even if Mom and Kelly hadn't exactly been the best of friends prior to the Airport Incident, they still rallied together in the name of principle. We might not have much in this family, but we have principle, we have the pugnacity of a drunken Irish boxer, and, whether we like it or not, we have each other.

Chapter 10:
Bad News

I set my alarm for three fifteen that morning; the van from the resort to the airport would be picking us up around four. I grumpily dragged myself out of bed, squelched across the damp floor to the bathroom, and got ready to leave. When I rolled my luggage into the lobby, I found my supervisor slumped over in an oversized armchair. I could hear his nose whistling as I approached. *"Oh, good. Please don't wake up."*

"Morning, Z." Damn.

"Good morning," I responded in that insincerely pleasant way I do whenever I've been awake for less than an hour.

"Ready to go back to Japan? I know I am," he mumbled, as if he'd just spent a week in the field in Afghanistan. I hadn't seen my supervisor but once – that time he forbade me from taking the most convenient, quickest, and cleanest route to work – and I can only assume that he spent the rest of his time in India downing pitchers of sangria at the resort pool and unsuccessfully hitting on rich European heiresses while I plodded through literal shit to fix broken and outdated shit.

"I guess so," I mumbled back. I was still bummed that I hadn't seen Arjun one more time before leaving, but my boss didn't need to know that an Indian family in the slums had adopted me as one of their own.

"Aw, did you meet yourself a cutie? I'm sure she has Facebook or WhatsApp, right?" I can appreciate that he had sensed the disappointment in my voice, but he was still a tool. "Speaking of which, let me message this honey real quick."

My boss started texting that hapless girl and I succumbed to the mighty Fear of Missing Out and pulled out my own phone. Once I was connected to WiFi I saw a notification for a private message on Facebook. It was from my cousin Helena. I hadn't spoken to her in almost a year, probably. "Hey Kevin, have you heard from Kyle recently? I can't get ahold of him."

Huh. Why would Helena, who lives less than twenty minutes away from Kyle in New Jersey, be asking if I, of all people, had heard from him? *"Oh yeah, his birthday's next month. Maybe she wants to ask for gift suggestions. But why would she ask me? I only ever get him something with a Beatle on it. But I am his brother, and brothers are supposed to know each other pretty well. Shit. I don't wanna tell her to just get him a mug with John Lennon's face on it. He's gotten enough of those from me."* I messaged her back: "Hey, Helena! The last time I heard from Kyle was on Christmas." It was May; I was only a little embarrassed. "Is everything okay? I'll send him a message right now."

No immediate response. Goa is nine and a half hours ahead of New Jersey, which made it about six thirty in the evening back home. *"I'm sure she's eating dinner right now. I'll see her response the next time I'm connected to WiFi, whenever that is."* The airport shuttle had pulled up outside the lobby and the driver was scurrying back and forth, loading up our bags. It was time to go. I turned off my phone, threw it back in my bag, and headed through the sliding glass doors. *"Shit, Kevin. You just told Helena you'd message Kyle right now."* I stopped on the curb and powered my phone back on.

"Yo, Z!" My supervisor was already in the front seat of the van with his feet propped up on the dashboard. "Let's go!"

"Be there in a sec! Family stuff!" I yelled back. WiFi was reconnected, Facebook was opening.

"Alright, man." He turned around to annoy our driver and fiddle with the radio knob. "You guys get any American music here? I can't do this Bollywood shit— 'stuff,' sorry."

"Alright…Where are you?" My brother wasn't anywhere on my list of recent contacts, and that thing goes back at least a year. I had to search his name, find his profile, and send him a message that way. I was honestly surprised we were still Facebook friends. "Hi, Kyle.

83

This is your brother. Helena's looking for you. Can you text or call her? Thanks."

And with that curt and impersonal message, sent like an email to a coworker I barely interact with, I shut off my phone for good and jumped in the van. As we headed for the airport, I could just barely make out the outline of the trash heaps lining either side of the highway. Every so often a bottle or aluminum can would catch the faint moonlight and break up the pitch-black monotony. I thought of Grandma and Arjun as I stared into the darkness, and I hoped he liked his chintzy little elephant. *"I'll look him up on Facebook. I'll search 'Arjun Goa' and see what pops up,"* I chuckled to myself. I still couldn't believe how much he looked like Kyle, and then I felt guilty for not even thinking to buy my brother a gift from the gift shop like I had Mom, Kelly, and, hell, an Indian kid whose name I wasn't even a hundred percent sure of. *"Should I have taken that elephant home for Kyle? No, he'd think it's stupid. And what would he say if I gave him a pineapple hair clip? I'll get him something with John and Yoko on it before I leave Japan."*

I realized that I would really miss Goa, and thought about all that I had enjoyed when I wasn't busy bitching about the *damp*, or the rude Europeans, or the walks through shit, or the squatting over stinky holes to poop when I was anywhere outside the comfort of the resort. The food and my adoptive family rotated between spots one and two on the list of things I'd miss the most. We arrived at the airport after a short ride, during which my boss asked cringeworthy questions like "What's that little dot for?" and "Do Indians not believe in wearing deodorant?" The driver was such an understanding man; I tipped him on behalf of all ignorant white people, knowing damn well that twenty bucks doesn't begin to cover that debt.

Lest I foolishly think that we'd be flying back to Japan in economy-class comfort, we actually walked *through* the airport to the military tarmac hidden in some far dark corner. There we met a group of U.S. Navy aircrewmen and their trusty EP-3 Orion aircraft, our shining chariot back to Japan and also a relic from a time when passengers could smoke in-flight and pilots took shots in the cockpit, also in-flight. My boss and I would be joining this crew on the first leg of their trip, from Goa to Yokosuka, before they'd continue on without us to Norfolk, Virginia. The plane's auxiliary power unit roared as maintainers scurried about, closing engine access panels, wiping down flight surfaces, and finishing up fueling operations in preparation for takeoff.

The crew was all decked out in their fancy leather flight jackets, and assembled on a set of bleachers on the side of the flight line like they were posing for a monochromatic J. Crew ad. The two of us, a pair of unglamorous, schlumpy maintainers, shuffled up to them and tried our best not to burst into tears at the sight of their coolness. In the Navy, maintainers and aircrewmen have a precarious relationship. Maintainers are constantly fixing these obsolete aluminum tubes and grumble when the aircrew inevitably returns them broken after a mission; the aircrewmen are constantly flying missions in these obsolete aluminum tubes and grumble when it inevitably takes maintainers a longer-than-anticipated time to fix them. It's a vicious and perpetual cycle of fixing, flying, breaking, fixing, and grumbling, and it makes for a fraught relationship.

"Yo." My supervisor's voice cracked and I heard giggles from some of the cool kids. I felt like a dweeb in high school all over again.

"You two ready?" the leader of the Jets asked in an effortfully uninterested tone. "Because *she's* ready." He nodded towards the plane and I expected him to rip the Ray-Ban aviators off his face like the guy from *CSI: Miami*.

"Yeah, man, we're *good to go*," my supervisor crossed his arms and cocked his head back.

"*Please just stop.*" Out of dirty maintainer camaraderie, I fought back the epic eye roll that my boss would have elicited under any other circumstances. "*Don't try to be a cool guy.*"

"Can we bring our bags up?" I asked, not for permission per se, but rather in an effort to surmount this impasse and get the flight over with. Once onboard, I shoved my bags into some out-of-the-way crevice, squeezed into a smelly, too-small secondhand flight vest, and payed attention – with as much interest as my exhaustion would allow – to the emergency instructions of an atypically friendly junior aircrewman.

"You're all set! Name's Putman, by the way, but everybody calls me 'Putty.'"

"Thanks, Putty. I'm Zalinsky, but everybody calls me 'Z.'"

And with that, we reached beyond our stations in life and tore down the barriers of class like a platonic Romeo and Juliet. Putty and I are still friends to this day.

"Um, you're probably going to have to sit on the floor by the main cabin door," Putty bashfully informed me. "Sorry! It's a full flight today."

"It's okay!" I didn't want my new friend and potential survival buddy to feel bad, so I helped her raise the plane's ladder and pull the cabin door shut. I was fully drenched in sweat at this point. "Yuck. I can't believe it's this hot already."

"I know! Too bad we can't cool off in that resort pool real quick, right?" Putty giggled, and I laughed along like I had any goddamn idea how that felt. *"Don't be bitter. You're almost out of here and you managed to make a friend."*

My spot on the floor was less a seat and more a hard metal flap with sharp edges and bolts that prodded my nether regions if I moved even slightly or if the plane made a sudden lurch. And that bird was in a lurching mood on this particular day. My feet kept sliding into the very narrow aisle and tripping aircrewmen as they hurried to and fro; I'd giggle every single time, but the dirty looks started to wear on me, plus I think they were intentionally stomping on my legs after a certain point. I stood up to give my legs and undercarriage some relief, and made my way to the kitchen in the back of the plane to find Putty. She was heating up a sandwich in a rusty, scarred toaster oven.

"Yikes! Careful not to set this whole thing on fire, Putty," I joked, but not really; that shivering hunk of metal hurtling through the air didn't offer much in the way of faith that we *wouldn't* plummet out of the sky and into a village in rural China.

"Don't worry, Z! A little kitchen fire is nothing!" Putty pointed at my terrified expression and laughed. "You're funny. We'll have any potential emergency under control, trust me."

"And we'll push you out of the way so you don't fuck anything up," a friendly aircrewman chirped at me from the booth across from the oven. I'm just kidding; he was actually a most unfriendly prick. He glared at me as if he were just *itching* for an emergency so he'd have an excuse to shove me headfirst into that hot oven. My nethers had already endured great pain, so I wasn't too scared of a little heat.

"Ha ha...thanks. So, Putty," I turned away from him and his unsettling gaze; I could feel his eyes boring through the back of my skull. "How long is this flight supposed to be?"

"Well, I *think* we have a layover in Thailand. Fingers crossed! Thailand's supposedly a lot of fun."

"Especially the ping pong shows," my pushy new friend barked over my shoulder.

"...Yuck. If we do," Putty continued, carefully removing her sandwich from the oven, "That's about nine hours. If we don't have a layover, that'll be about twelve. But all signs point to 'yes!'"

"I had no idea you got so excited over ping pong shows, Putty," Pushy joked. My supervisor, who was sprawled out across both seats opposite Pushy, began stirring upon mention of the infamous Thai ping pong show.

"Don't be gross. They have a *huge* golden Buddha there that I'd love to see! Have you ever been, Z? You should come with!"

"Sure thing! That sounds awesome," I happily accepted Putty's offer and returned to my "seat" as she returned to hers. I sat down, careful not to plop directly onto a protruding screw – I didn't know how current my tetanus shot was. I pulled my legs in and sat cross-legged, leaning up against the ladder and praying that the cabin door didn't fly open. I closed my eyes and started to nod off. The last thing I remember hearing was my boss, still in the back of the plane, squealing with delight like a horny teenage boy attending his very first ping pong show: "Yo, dude, I can't wait!"

When I woke up a few hours later, crew members were still hurrying up and down the tube, but were now careful to step *over* my legs which had since slipped back into the aisle. They weren't even giving me dirty looks; instead, they'd *smile*, however halfheartedly, at me as they gingerly moved by. "*Alright, Putty!*" I thought she must have put in a good word for me. "*See? Maintainers aren't so bad,*" I'd telepathically gloat as they'd pass.

The pilot, who I had seen only once, when we boarded the plane, came over the loudspeaker to announce that we would not be stopping in Thailand after all. "Aw, that's too bad," I mumbled to myself. "So much for the giant golden Buddha." I peeked out from behind the ladder to see if anybody else was reacting to the news. Nobody so much as shook their head or groaned. "Huh. They all must have already known." I caught Putty's eye, and at least she wore a commiserating half-smile. "*I'm sorry,*" she mouthed.

With that bit of disappointing news, I returned my head to its pillow of a metal ladder rung and was shaken back to sleep by the incessant lurching for the remainder of the flight. I was jolted awake when our obsolete aluminum tube landed with a rattling thud in Yokosuka. "*Phew! We made it.*" I stood up and pressed myself against the bulkhead to stay out of the way as the aircrewmen carried out their post-flight duties. There wasn't much in the way of chatter; there was a weird vibe in the air. I was sure everyone was just as exhausted as I was. Somebody I hadn't met had opened the cabin door and was busy dropping the ladder. "Hey, Putty. What are you responsible for after a flight?" I asked as she flitted past. "I can help!"

"Oh…Thanks, Z, but you don't have to help. I'm in charge of the pisser." On the EP-3, the entire crew pees into a giant plastic urinal which is stained with and reeks of decades of urine, and is affectionately referred to as "the pisser."

"I don't mind! That thing is probably really heavy. I don't want you to have to carry it down the ladder and through the hangar by yourself."

"Thanks, Z…That would be a big help. Be right back." Putty ran up to the flight station to tell the pilot some quick thing, pointing towards the back of the plane as she spoke, and then met me outside the lavatory. "Are you ready for this?"

"Yeah!" I was most certainly not ready. That thing had been freshly topped off, and it was *heavy*. With every step down the aircraft's very steep ladder, I'd hear its contents sloshing around and feared I'd be splashed in the face with twenty-four distinct brands of urine mixed together into one frothy brew. "Do you do this after *every* flight, Putty?"

"Yeah, but I usually have to carry it down by myself. You're really a big help, Z."

It was around two in the morning, but I didn't know what day it was. "*We left India at five thirty on Sunday, so maybe it's Monday? Surely it isn't already Tuesday?*" Tuesday was my one day off a week, and I didn't want to sleep away my precious free hours in the barracks. It didn't really matter – the exhaustion had made me so giddy that I was practically skipping through the hangar as we lugged the pisser to the bathroom. The night shift was working then, which meant my best friend Kendall would be around somewhere. I reminded myself that I had to go see her and tell her all about India – after washing my hands, of course.

Santiago sort of half-waved at me as I passed. Stevenson, toolbox in hand, stopped dead in her tracks with a clatter and stared. A few maintainers from the electronics division looked up from their circuit cards and multimeters and started talking in hushed voices. In my periphery, I could see people circling us at a great distance, as if we were performing high kicks while balancing an uncovered pisser on our heads. "*Is it just me, or is everyone acting weird?*" I rhetorically asked myself. My mind was swirling with delirium; I felt like I was floating through a dream. *"Am I still fast asleep against that ladder?"*

"Huh." I looked over at Putty. Her jaw was clenched and she was staring straight ahead. I hadn't known her for very long, but even so, I didn't think it was possible for her to look so solemn. "What's up, Putty?"

"Nothing, Z. Nothing at all," she said, glancing at me and very obviously forcing a smile. She grabbed her handle with both hands, as if she were worried she'd drop her side of the pisser. *"Is she about to cry? No, she's just tired. I can't wait 'til I can crawl into bed. Will they keep me at work, or let me go sleep, I wonder?"*

"Well, here we are! I think we should go into the female head; I don't want you to see what the male head looks like…or smells like," I chuckled. We had passed through the double doors which separated the hangar from the admin offices and bathrooms, and put the pisser down, careful as ever not to spill. The water fountains were right there, after all.

"I've got it from here, Z. Thank you so much for your help. I'm sorry we couldn't go see the golden Buddha together." I could no longer delude myself into thinking that Putty was just tired. Tears were spilling out of her eyes and onto the front of her flight suit. She looked over my shoulder, down the long hallway towards the executive suite. I heard footsteps on the linoleum tile behind me and turned to see none other than my commanding officer, marching down the hall in our direction.

"Why is the CO at work at two o'clock in the morning?" I immediately sensed that something was very, very wrong. *"What did I do?"* I panicked. *"I must be in deep shit."*

"Petty Officer Zalinsky, how are you doing this morning?" I didn't have time to answer. "I'm afraid I have some bad news for you." His expression was grave; his typically bright eyes were bleary.

Suddenly, it all made sense. The all-but-guaranteed Thailand layover being cancelled. The aircrewmen smiling at me and taking care not to trample my legs. Putty running up to talk to the pilot about "pisser duty," and then becoming increasingly distraught as we walked through the hangar. My coworkers, most of whom were also my good friends, acting weird or outright avoiding me as I passed by. Helena's Facebook message. That should've been the first red flag. I ignored it. I shouldn't have been so quick to turn off my phone and jump in that shuttle. I ran away. She hadn't been able to get in touch with Kyle. *Kyle? This is about Kyle.*

"This is about my brother, isn't it?" I knew, right then and there, before my commanding officer had even answered me. My gut twisted, my knees buckled, I lost my balance and collapsed against the concrete wall. The pungent smell of urine filled my nostrils and I retched. I turned my head to see Kendall running towards me as my vision narrowed. I could hear her yelling my name, but her voice was muffled. Everything had become so blurry and indistinct. Something had been gnawing at me since I woke up in Goa, but I distracted myself with exhaustion and my annoying boss and roaring engines and rattling metal and being in the way and staying out of the way and latching onto a new friend. I remember feeling my throat tighten and the hot tears streaming down my cheeks. I remember pressing my forehead against the wall and realizing that I wouldn't be able to feel that cool concrete if I were dreaming. I remember how everything felt in that moment, the moment I knew that my brother was dead.

Chapter 11:
Past Lives and New Love

"Kyle, are you sure this thing can get us to the City?" I skeptically surveyed my brother's "new" 1994 Toyota Camry. I'm no car snob, but this was a far cry from Dad's Ford Focus which Kyle ran into the ground back in September 2002. It was a balmy May evening and the air was sweet with honeysuckle. "*I guess this isn't a terrible night to die.*"

"What do you mean, 'this thing?' She's a great car! She'll get us there, no problem." Kyle was beaming with pride; he bought the car outright with three hundred dollars cash and named it Sexy Sadie. My brother had apparently become a master of irony in the year or so since I'd last seen him.

"Okay...but can she get us *back*?" As excited as I was to go into New York for the evening, I was equally *not* excited about the prospect of being stranded on the side of the parkway with Kyle.

"Stop worrying so much. Don't you trust me?" Kyle and I had been making substantial progress on our quest for a better relationship. I didn't want to bungle it by telling him the truth, so I just nodded my head. Lies can't be nonverbal, can they?

The last time Kyle and I had gone on a road trip together, he all but forced me to come out to him. I had since developed mixed feelings about the experience. On the one hand, he kicked open the closet door to declare his unwavering support and his heroic willingness to "be there;" on the other hand, had he even bothered to consider that maybe I wasn't ready? Because I most certainly was *not* ready. I wasn't ready to become someone's token gay friend. I wasn't ready to answer inane questions like "Are you more of a Will, or more of a Jack?" (I'm actually mostly a Karen.) I wasn't ready to have the entirety of my existence condensed into an insufferable "yas queen." I wasn't ready to have to explain or theorize something that just *is*, like my blood type just *is* or my penicillin allergy just *is*. Nobody should ever feel rushed or pressured to come out, just like nobody should ever be confronted in a moving car with no alternative other than to tuck and roll out onto a rural highway in the middle of the Pine Barrens. I'm sure the Jersey Devil is a raging homophobe. It doesn't matter how "obvious" it may be, and there's a phrase about good intentions being put to clever use by the Department of Transportation of the Dominion of Hell.

Still, I recognized my comparatively fortunate circumstances. He hadn't kicked open the closet door to beat the shit out of me, after all. At that point in my life, Kyle was the only person I had come out to, voluntarily or otherwise. I'm not sure he ever realized just how important that made him to me.

"Alright, so Claudia is gonna be there tonight. Don't fuck this up for me," he warned, as if I had even the slightest interest in his love life or sexual escapades. I had exactly zero interest in those things. One time, he started talking about cunnilingus and I vomited all over the kitchen floor before collapsing in said vomit.

"Since when do you like Claudia?"

Claudia was in the same class as Kyle, and she happened to live three houses down from us on Glenn Avenue. He terrorized this poor girl for twelve years. He'd put a freshly-chewed wad of gum on her seat at lunchtime, and then scream "Look, everyone! Claudia has shit on her ass!" when she got up to clear off her tray. He'd push her books off the desk and onto the floor, but not before tying her pigtails to the back of her chair. Every day after school in the month of December, Kyle would walk past Claudia's house and loosen a random bulb so *none* of the Christmas lights would turn on.

Kyle celebrated the birth of our Lord and Savior not by raising his voice on high in exultant worship, not by spreading goodwill and cheer for his fellow man to hear, not even by listening to the Muppets squawk along with John Denver, but by disrupting the neighbors' small-scale light show. Claudia's mom eventually caught onto his little game. One day, as Kyle was picking out the perfect bulb, she threw open the front door, sending their wreath flying across the porch, and yelled "I *knew* it was you!" Kyle raced home, but Claudia's mom wasn't far behind. Mom was just getting home from work when she was confronted. "Do you know what *your son* has been up to?"

"I just got home from work! What do *you* think the answer to that question is?" Mom curbed her sass once she noticed how frazzled Claudia's mom was. "What did he do now?"

"He walks past my house *every day* and unscrews one of my Christmas lights! My husband has to check *all of them* after work so we can turn them on!"

"Oh." I think Mom was expecting a report involving small animals or a flaming bag of dog poop. Her expression must have said "*He's doing you a favor; those lights are a fucking eyesore.*"

"Well?! What are you going to do about it?!" By this point Claudia's Mom was one "ack!" away from a *Cathy* cartoon.

"I am going to talk to him as soon as I get out of my work clothes, get dinner started, and pour myself a glass of wine."

"You *working mothers* are all the same," she snapped. "You never know where your kids are or what they're up to!"

"Hey! I know where my kids are at every second of every day! So why don't you bring your stay-at-home ass *back home* and fix your goddamn lights?" Mom slammed the front door in Claudia's mom's face. I was just proud she hadn't pushed her down the porch steps first. She marched into the house to find me and Dad cowering in the kitchen. "Where's Kyle?"

Dad and I looked at each other and responded, in unison, "I don't know."

"I've always had a thing for Claudia. I just teased her a little bit," Kyle explained, waving off the years of terrorism and light-loosening.

"Well, she was actually my friend. Do you know how hard it was for us to be friends with *you* as my brother?" I met Claudia when I joined the theater club in high school. I was a freshman newbie, and she was a seasoned thespian junior. I didn't look too much like Kyle in those days, so I was able to hide my relation to him until she discovered my last name. "*Shit. She's going to hate me.*" Luckily for me, Claudia understood that the Curse of Thorn affects only one son of the damned family, and we were able to become good friends. We still are, to this day; we often lovingly reminisce over the ways Kyle tormented us and made our lives miserable.

"Yeah, yeah. She was totally into me." Kyle's considerable charm had afforded him a comfortable level of delusion. "Alright, let's get going."

I should have known right then and there that we'd be in for quite a night: in order to get the car started, Kyle had to punch the ignition as he shifted from park to neutral, while I pushed the car out of the driveway. I then had to jump in the front seat as the car rolled backwards and Kyle shifted first from neutral to reverse, and then from reverse to drive. If all went well, Sadie would be tricked into operating like a normally-functioning car; if not, well, at least Mom didn't live on a cliff or next to any major highways. "Good job! We should only have to do that one more time tonight."

The City is about an hour away from Dunellen, the town we moved to after Kyle got expelled from the Union County Public School System and Mom and Dad had to pay for him to go to a private school for scoundrels. Or whatever they were calling it. Sadie sputtered and groaned on the way, but only if Kyle drove over fifty miles per hour, or if he turned on the air conditioning, or if he idled at a red light, or if he used the blinker. Otherwise, smooth sailing!

The drive was much less awkward than our previous road trip; Kyle mercifully cranked the volume up to exempt us from any excruciating small talk. He'd ask, "Do you like this?" during the four-second break between songs, and I'd reply "Yeah!" during the next break. Kyle introduced me to *Under the Blacklight* by Rilo

Kiley on that trip, and he confessed to me that its Seventies pastiche had all but confirmed his suspicions that he had been born in the wrong era. He was convinced that he should have been doing coke in Los Angeles while waiting in line for a Fleetwood Mac concert after getting drunk with hookers on Dan Fogelberg's yacht, and all I could do was snort and roll my eyes.

I may have acted unimpressed, but I was actually jealous of Kyle. Not the cocaine and hookers part, but the fact that thoughts like those had even crossed his mind. I never considered that I might have been born in the wrong era, or who I might have been in a past life, or that I might have been cool enough to be invited to a yacht party. I barely know who I am in the present. I've always had a feeling that I don't know myself very well. I put up barriers to keep people at a safe distance, and in doing so I hold even myself at bay. My relationships have always suffered because of it; my relationship with Kyle was no different.

"Can you loosen up a little bit?" He looked over at me, arms crossed and leaning as far away from him as physically possible. The side of my face was practically pressed up against the glass of the window. "You don't look like you're having any fun."

"I am! I'm having fun." I must have been worried that Satan would make an overdue appearance. I hadn't spent time with Kyle in quite a while, and it felt like I was riding in a car with a stranger. By then, I had been in the Navy for almost three years, and our lives were continuing on with very little in the way of overlap. I didn't know that he had quit one band in the middle of a gig to form another one with his girlfriend – he didn't find my Yoko Ono jokes very funny – and he thought I had joined the Navy to be an engine mechanic. His eyes would gloss over whenever I'd try to explain the basics of avionics to him. "Uh huh" is the most I ever heard from him when I talked about work.

"Here." He scrounged around in the pocket of his leather jacket for something. "Have this." He handed me a piece of chocolate.

"Just one piece?" The Navy may have melted away the pounds, but I was still an incorrigible fatty at heart.

"One piece is all you need, trust me." I took the little square from his palm and eyed it suspiciously. Kyle, sensing my apprehension, assured me, "It's not a laxative, or poison, or anything that can kill you. Just eat it."

I sniffed it. It smelled a little weird, but not like poop. *"Would Kyle really keep poop in his pocket just for the off chance to prank me?"* I cautiously nibbled a corner of it to verify its authenticity, and it seemed like the genuine article. "Okay…" It really was chocolate. I ate it, and it wasn't long before my gums started to feel numb, my tongue tingled, and my teeth were pirouetting in their sockets.

"That's THC chocolate. It just takes the edge off. You already seem so much more relaxed."

"Oh, THC cho—" I nearly choked on my tingly tongue. "THC chocolate?! Kyle, I'm in the Navy! I can't get high!"

"Calm down. You're home for a month, right? It'll be *way* out of your system by the time you go back." I wanted to be furious at his nonchalance, but I was giggling too much. One can't possibly take a giggling grown man seriously. I threw my head back against the seat and melted into a chortling puddle of titters. Kyle broke off two pieces for himself and tossed them back. "Don't worry, by the time it hits me we'll be halfway through dinner."

Thankfully my giggling fit was over and my teeth had stopped dancing by the time we met up with Claudia and another friend from high school theater club, Vincenza. "Oh. My. *God.* Look at the Zalinsky Brothers!" Claudia exclaimed in her best impression of the white girl from Sir Mix-a-Lot's *Baby Got Back* as we walked into the pizza place. "My darling Kevin, and…*Kyle.*"

"Hi there!" I gave Claudia a big hug, and remembered that the last time we had embraced was when we were dance partners in *West Side Story*. Claudia has always referred to me as her *favorite* terrible dance partner. "Long time no see, stranger!" I gave Vincenza a hug as Kyle and Claudia faced off after a seven-year break in combat engagements.

"Hey, Claudia," Kyle said in an uncharacteristically sheepish voice. "I brought you something." From his other, non-chocolate pocket, he pulled out a partial string of Christmas lights like a birthday clown with handkerchiefs. Never mind, same old Kyle.

"You are *such* an asshole!" Claudia couldn't help but double over with laughter at the absurd sight. Like me, it was hard for her to be mad at Kyle. I wondered if *that's* what it felt like to be his friend on any given day, and not just his punching bag or an unfortunate casualty of his mood swings. "Give me a hug, Lucifer."

"'Lucifer Zalinsky!' Why didn't *I* ever think of that? It has the perfect ring to it!" I had long since settled on "Satan" but felt a change coming on. It was a shame Kyle had been acting far less devilish lately.

"Hmm…I don't remember 'Lucifer,'" Vincenza put her index finger on her chin as she pretended to ponder, "But I *do* recall 'Kyle Zalinsky just looked at me! He's so cute! I mean…for a total jerk.'"

Claudia and Kyle both started to blush. She pulled the string of lights out of his hand and mimed hanging herself. "I would *never* say that!"

"See, Kev, I told you: she totally had a thing for me." Claudia then mimed strangling Kyle with a little more believability in her performance.

The four of us sat there for hours, laughing, drinking, eating greasy pepperoni pizza, sharing memories, gossiping about old classmates, and catching up. Claudia was a stand-up comedienne and aspiring actress who had landed a few commercial spots; Vincenza spritzed perfume during the day while her drag queen alter ego sashayed and slayed after nightfall; I had joined the Navy and was living in Hawaii; and Kyle was his usual charming self. I remember looking across the table at him and seeing not my tormentor, not my nemesis, but my *brother*. He was beaming as I told Claudia and Vincenza all about my life post-high school, and I don't think it was solely because of the funny chocolate. Not after the first two hours, anyway. Years later, Claudia would recall just how excited Kyle was on that night that I was not only home, but had voluntarily agreed to spend time with him.

When I returned to the table from the restroom, I noticed Kyle smirking as I pulled out my chair. "What?" I checked for a chewed-up wad of gum before I took my seat.

"Nothing," he replied, in the way someone says "nothing" when they most certainly mean "something." Claudia and Vincenza exchanged a knowing glance and turned their heads down with a giggle.

"The Zalinsky Brothers!" Claudia gasped, as if encountering a pair of infamous creatures from ancient lore. "You know, I don't think I've *ever* seen the two of you getting along like this before. I could never have imagined you laughing and…not killing each other."

"What's so surprising about it?" Kyle put his hands behind his head and rocked his chair back. "Kevin's my brother and I love him."

"That must be great to hear," Vincenza said, in a near whisper, as she turned her face from the others to look me in the eye. Hers were welling up, just a tiny bit. She must have sensed it: that was the first time I had ever heard Kyle say anything remotely close to "I love you" in my twenty-four years of life.

"Hey, while we're in Brooklyn, I need to go *here*." I handed Kyle a folded sticky note as we made our way back to Sadie.

"A bakery? We just ate all that pizza, Kevin."

"I just want to take a picture there for…*a friend*. He grew up around here and his family apparently went to this bakery all the time."

"A 'friend,' huh?" Kyle smirked. "Alright, I get it. It should be close."

"Thanks." My brother's senses of direction and navigation were unrivaled, probably from years of having to make quick getaways after causing mischief of one kind or another.

"So…this…'friend'…"

"*Goddammit.*" He was my boyfriend at the time, ex-boyfriend now. Well, ex-boyfriend nine ex-boyfriends ago.

"Does he treat you right? Because I'll fly to Hawaii to kick a motherfucker's ass if I have to. Tell him your big brother said that."

Chapter 12:
Drunk on Delusion

"My name is Kevin, and I'm an alcoholic."

It would be years before I'd actually believe those words when I said them. I dragged my feet into Alcoholics Anonymous more begrudgingly than even the court-ordered attendees. I pouted, I crossed my arms, I avoided eye contact, I never donated, not even spare change, and I most certainly never shared my story. I was convinced that I "didn't belong" in Alcoholics Anonymous; it would be a long time before that Solo cup of delusion juice was slapped out of my hand and I wouldn't scramble for a re-up.

"My name is Jerry, and I'm an alcoholic."

"Hi, Jerry!" Came the supportive chorus as I rolled my eyes like a jerk.

"Today, I'm six months sober," Jerry said to rapt applause and cries of "Good job, Jerry!" from the choir. "Today is also my sixty-fourth birthday."

My ears perked up. *Dad would've been sixty-four.*" I am always keenly aware of how old Dad would be if he were still alive, same as with Kyle and MeeMaw. I looked at Jerry; his was the face of a much older man. He had heavy bags under his eyes and deep creases which formed trenches across his forehead. His skin was about as gray as his hair, which was sharply parted and neatly combed. I could tell his face was handsome under the weather and wear. "*Just like Dad.*" Jerry's eyes, however, were nothing like Dad's. They seemed so heavy and defeated, dragged down by the weight of every unpleasant thing they had ever seen. They were so *sad*. Jerry had a huge gut, also unlike Dad, which he rested on the back of his chair when he stood and turned to face his audience. I could just imagine Mom fixating on that gut while Jerry spoke and muttering "yech" just barely under her breath.

"This chip," Jerry choked up as he held up his yellow six-month sobriety chip, "is the best thing to happen to me in…in years."

"*How sad,*" I thought to myself, conveniently forgetting that the last six months of my own life hadn't exactly been a walk in the park. I had, after all, ended up at the very same Alcoholics Anonymous meeting as this Jerry. Oh, but I "didn't belong" there.

"I can admit, without embarrassment, that I'm an old man. I'm wrinkly, I'm heavy, I'm tired. I can also freely admit that I'm an alcoholic," Jerry announced to more enthusiastic applause; admitting the problem is the first step to dealing with the problem, after all. "What I *am* ashamed to admit…" Jerry's voice and my heart cracked in unison. "…is that I'm a lousy husband and father."

I took a swig of coffee and bit down on the lip of my Styrofoam cup. I hadn't prepared myself at all for dealing with heavy stuff at these meetings. I had assumed that people show up a few minutes late, hand in their attendance sheets for a signature, get some free bad coffee, and play on their phones while absentmindedly reciting some rules of sobriety. For the sake of my well-being, I had to immediately stop thinking of the ways in which Jerry reminded me of Dad. I had heard Dad's voice crack, like Jerry's just had, only once in my entire life, and it was a devastating thing.

I had driven Dad to what would become one of his last few chemotherapy appointments. We were heading home, and *(Sittin' on) The Dock of the Bay* was playing on the car radio. I tried to distract Dad from that morning's treatment, to cheer him up even a little bit, by telling him that we'd go on road trip to San Francisco once he was better, that we'd find that spot where Otis Redding sat as he watched the tide roll away. He turned his head with a great strain to look at me and said, feebly, "That sounds nice, Kevin." His voice broke, and all I could do was turn away from him, like a coward, to survey all the nothing out the driver's side window. My eyes stung so sharply I thought I'd go blind. I relented and let the tears fall only when I saw, in my periphery, Dad's head slump down into his chest. Dad napped, I sobbed, and, because the universe apparently has a dark and very literal sense of humor, *Tears in Heaven* played next on the radio.

"I spent my whole life living for just one person: myself," Jerry continued, pulling me out of that dismal memory.

"Listen to Jerry, Kevin. Don't think about Dad right now. For God's sake, just listen to Jerry."

I realized I must have been the only person in that room who was actually paying attention to him. Others busied themselves with refilling their bad coffee at the snack table, or looking at the sad inspirational posters slapped crookedly on the walls, or staring out the window of that community center folding chair storage room. As alluring as Jerry's belly was, it couldn't really compete with Hawaii. I'm sure *"Why am I stuck inside listening to this guy's sob story when I could be out there?"* was running through more than one person's head. Still, I gave Jerry my attention; there were only ten minutes left before I could grab my attendance sheet and haul ass out of there.

"I never thought of anyone but me, not even my own family. When my oldest daughter graduated from high school, I was in a bar. When my middle daughter left for her junior prom, I was drunk and passed out in the basement. My son played his first college ball game; I was upside-down in my car on the side of the road. At least I tried to make it to that one," Jerry said to uneasy chuckles from the group. "And…when my son was leaving voicemails on my phone…when he was calling me to…to tell me that he was thinking of…ending his life…" Jerry covered his eyes with one hand and grabbed the back of his chair with the other. "Where was I? I was lying facedown in an alley behind some bar. My phone was under a dumpster. I must have kicked it there as I passed out. I missed *every single one* of my son's phone calls."

"Oh, my God. That's terrible." This was at least a year before "suicide" had forced its way into my regular vocabulary, before it had blown an irreparable hole in the hull of my family's already-leaking lifeboat.

Jerry ran his calloused hands down his face, wiping away tears and revealing those eyes, full to bursting with sadness. A woman in the front row jumped up and embraced him, pulling away to dab more tears from his cheeks. Other members of the group shouted affirmations and rallied around Jerry, taking turns for their birthday and six-months-sober hugs. If they hadn't been fully invested in his story a moment earlier, he couldn't escape their attentions now. It was a strangely beautiful thing to bear witness to, and I struggled in vain to not feel anything.

Jerry finished sharing once the hugging had concluded: "*Thank you*. You all remind me that…I might have been a bad husband, and a bad father, but…by working the steps and working on myself, there's a chance for me to make things right with my family. I can't change the past – it's too late for that – but I sure can work hard to make the…however many years I have left…good ones."

Jerry took his seat to chants of "Jerry! Jerry!" and "Keep coming back, it works, it works!" as I took another gulp from my Styrofoam cup and looked around at anything and everything but Jerry. I couldn't avoid him for long.

"Hi there, young man." Jerry cornered me at the chairperson's table after I had slunk up to grab my attendance sheet. I was trapped between the table and Jerry's gut; there was no escape. "I've never seen you here before. First-timer?"

"Uh…yep!" I held up the sheet in front of my face and shook it, as if to say "*Please don't eat me! I'm only here for a signature!*"

"Ahh, I remember those days," Jerry said as he inched closer to me, forcing me to sidle towards the wall with my ass pressed up against the front of the table, ruffling other peoples' papers as I went. "Come to two meetings a week, get your signatures, figure out how to forge those signatures, stop coming to the meetings, get your two hours a week back," Jerry chuckled as he turned his head to survey my face with what I assumed was his "truth-finding eye." I blushed; he was on to me like I'm sure he was on to *every* twenty-something who occasionally popped up on his turf. He was a sharp man, that Jerry.

"Forge signatures? Me?" I scoffed very unconvincingly. "No way! I'll be back next week!" Now, on principle, I *had* to go to those two meetings a week. Mom would be so very proud of her alcoholic son.

"Glad to hear it, Son. I wish I had had meetings like these when I was your age. They would've done me a world of good." Normally, I spastically cringe and my eyes roll clean out of my head whenever I hear the beginning of a "Back in my day…" yarn, but Jerry didn't irritate me for some reason. He seemed like a very genuine, caring person. Having heard his heartbreaking backstory, I was able to keep my obnoxious whippersnapper attitude in check. "Now, what's your name? If you don't mind my asking. I didn't hear you say it today."

"Of course not," I responded. I shook Jerry's hand when he extended it. It was very rough, but at least the tears had dried. "I'm Kevin."

"Very nice to meet you, Kevin. Hopefully you'll recall that I'm Jerry. Can we expect to hear your story sometime?"

"*Sometime*, sure." Jerry struck me as the kind of guy who would never forget that somebody had agreed in passing and with great hesitation to do something. I knew I was on the hook to share in front of this roomful of strangers at some point. Thankfully, Jerry wouldn't again broach the subject until I came to the meeting one week and told him I was ready to talk. But that would take quite some time.

In the meantime, I resisted the urge to forge chairperson Gayle's signature – she signed her initials in big bubble cursive, like a second grader using beginner's lined paper, which just begged to be duplicated – and I gradually uncrossed my arms and started throwing my spare change into the donation basket. I still drank at least two cups of bad coffee at every meeting, but I found myself brewing more Maxwell House if I noticed the pot getting low. Everyone at that meeting, myself included, had found a new addiction to supplant their old one: the twitches and jitters were not from alcohol withdrawal, but rather from caffeine overload.

Eventually, I stopped trying to convince myself that I "didn't belong" there, and I embraced my new identity as one of "those people."

Kendall, who would later wrap her arms around me in the tightest hug to keep me from crumbling to pieces, accompanied me to more than a few meetings for support. To ask anyone to give up an entire Hawaiian hour to sit through an Alcoholics Anonymous meeting, when they could just as easily be doing nothing in Hawaii, is a big ask. But Kendall would always act as if I hadn't asked for a thing. She'd put on a big smile, make-believe her friend wasn't a complete and utter mess, and treat that meeting like it were any other day trip on the island. We lived next door to each other in the barracks; I'd leave my room to go knock on her door, only to find her waiting outside and ready to go hang out with a roomful of alcoholics.

"Kevin, you ain't no alcoholic," Kendall would inform me, almost every single time we walked up to the front doors of that community center. "You're just sad about what happened to your daddy. Hell, I'd be an 'alcoholic' too if I lost my daddy like that."

"Well, it's one thing to be sad, but to get *that sad* when I drink? It's scary, Kendall." In those meetings, I had heard, over and over and over again, not to blame our troubles with alcohol on outside influences or past experiences, no matter how traumatizing. I tried, with varying degrees of difficulty and delusion, to adopt that mindset as my own. I'm still trying.

Kendall stopped in her tracks and sucked her teeth. "Kevin, you ain't like these people here. Some of these stories I've heard..." she trailed off as she shook her head. "What about that lady who got in the wrong car at Burger King and then *drove into a church*? Or that dude who blacked out and woke up in a damn chicken coop? You ain't never done shit like that!"

"Well, those are some pretty extreme scenarios...But I'm sure they started off small. Who's to say I won't wind up like them if I don't get help now?"

"I'm mad that you have to go to two of these damn meetings every week because of *those* assholes. *They* were picking a fight with *you*. You didn't call *them* terrible names! *They* need help; *you* need to be left alone."

"Kendall, *I love you* for defending me," I put my hands on the elbows of Kendall's crossed arms and looked her in the eye. "But all that…that's on me. I know those guys said shitty things to me, but that's not what worries me. I don't like the things I was thinking, the ways I was feeling…It was bad."

"Uh-uh, I'm not buying it. You *know* it's wrong. All those motherfuckers need to be here, *not* you!" She uncrossed her arms and gestured in every general direction at these unspecified "motherfuckers."

I had never seen Kendall so livid that her eyes had teared up. Even on that night she had been alluding to, with her talk of wrongness and motherfuckers, she wasn't *this* upset. I can recall, with surprising clarity given my ludicrous drunkenness at the time, how she had torn open her door upon hearing howls of "faggot this" and "faggot that;" how she had marched from the third floor of the barracks down to the open courtyard to find the source of these slurs; how she had found me, lying on a bench, sobbing, slobbering, and missing a shoe; and how she had confronted Big D – an obnoxious nickname for an obnoxious bro – with "Now don't *make me* embarrass you in front of your little friends, because I *will* kick your ass!"

D muttered under his breath as Kendall pulled me to my feet and yanked my missing shoe out of a bush. As she pushed her weeping, stumbling mess of a best friend towards the stairs, she yelled back over her shoulder, "If I hear any of y'all use *that word* around Kevin *ever again*…stand the fuck by!" And, for good measure, once we finally made it to the third floor and D and his cronies were still smarting from that string of verbal beatdowns: "Stay the *fuck* away from my best friend!"

Kendall steered me in the direction of my bed as I came crashing down. She brought me a bottle of water to chug and four ibuprofens to take before I fell asleep. She told me not to be sad, not to worry about a thing, that I'd feel much better in the morning, that my troubles would be millions of miles away by the time I woke up. Unfortunately, there would be no such galactic expanse separating me from my woes. The military police had received several noise complaints regarding the Navy barracks, and, in this case, not even Kendall herself could offer a convincing argument in my defense.

I appreciated Kendall for her fierce protection and her unwavering devotion, but I made those choices. I *chose* to drink the Budweiser, and the Sailor Jerry, and the shots of whatever liquor was mixed together into that ungodly concoction. I *chose* to hang out in close proximity to known assholes and suspected homophobes. Alcohol can't make friends out of adversaries, it can't wash away toxic masculinity, and it can't drown homophobia. I was tired of blaming others, even when I had a scapegoat as convenient as Big D. And, although my behavior on that night landed me in hot water and two Alcoholics Anonymous meetings a week, it still wasn't *the* issue. Dad had been gone for more than three years at that point, and I was no closer to closure than I had been on the morning of March 11th, 2006.

My theory, as the highly unqualified and wildly misinformed amateur analyzer of human behavior that I am, is that I was delaying my confrontation with Dad's death by busying myself with *stuff*. But when the list of *stuff* was all checked off, when the evening crept up on me and wrapped me in its quiet melancholy, I had nothing to distract me from my thoughts. Dad would step out of the shadows of my mind's periphery in that cool way of his and just smile as if to ask, "Are you ready to deal with me, Son?" I never was, so I'd go out. Not to a bar or a club or anything, but literally outside my room, where I'd find the usual barracks gang. And I'd drink. Whatever they were drinking; I wasn't picky in my flight from emotional maturity. We'd drink almost every night – I heard *Friends in Low Places* more times than any one person should hear in an entire lifetime – and I'm still not sure how any of us sustained that demanding regularity. It's not like any of us had much in common besides work, which, to be fair, provided at least four hours' worth of bitching every night.

When the twenty-four pack of Pabst Blue Ribbon was finished – don't judge us; we were all a little broken and a lot sad – we'd retreat, with varying degrees of difficulty, to our respective barracks rooms and crash mere hours before our phone alarms would rudely remind us of our stupid adult obligations. On a good night, I'd stumble into my room and somehow manage to remove both shoes and connect my phone to the charger before collapsing in bed, or at least on the floor next to it. I didn't think, I didn't feel, I didn't analyze, I didn't reminisce – I slept. And then I'd wake, grumble to myself about how shitty I felt and how stupid I was to drink like that on a weeknight, and I'd go about my day, checking off my list of *stuff*.

I didn't have very many good nights. Dad would be waiting for me in that cramped, dingy room on the not-so-good ones. No, that's far too sinister of a statement to associate at all with Dad. The specter of my guilt, my failure, my resentment, my anger, my agony – *it* waited for me in the shadows of that room, creeping along the walls and grabbing me by the back of the neck just as the doorknob to the safe haven of sleep was within my grasp.

It was like the first time I had seen *Halloween*. I must have been nine; Kyle came home from Blockbuster with a stack of scary movies: *Psycho*, *A Nightmare on Elm Street*, *Friday the 13th*, *Black Christmas*, and, what the two of us would soon discover to be the pinnacle of low-budget, high-scares horror, *Halloween*. Kyle had begged Mom all week for permission to pick out his own rentals during our routine Friday night trip to the video store. She allowed it, only after Kyle had loaded the dishwasher every night after dinner, demonstrated his ability to restrain the compulsion to terrorize his little brother, and, of course, paid with his own money. Kyle feigned kindness when he allowed me to accompany him on this carnival ride of horror, but really, I think he didn't want to be alone in the dark of the basement TV room and *any* company would do. Thus was I introduced to Michael Myers and the stark white, emotionless, terrifying mask of the Boogeyman.

For months after I had watched him stalk Laurie Strode, strangle Annie Brackett from the backseat of her car, and impale that poor doofus with a kitchen knife and watch him die, I couldn't close my eyes to fall asleep without seeing that mask. He'd be watching me from behind that rubber visage, and, even if I reminded myself that it was just a William Shatner mask spray-painted white, that face haunted me. It had imprinted itself on the insides of my eyelids. I'd close my eyes, and there he was. I'd squeeze them tight to force him out, only to see the same mask with inverted colors when my eyes inevitably sprang open.

It was the same thing with Dad, only it happened when I was drunk. His face – cold, unsmiling, unfriendly, entirely void of color – was there, on the backs of my eyelids. It was as if Michael Myers had gotten fed up with the William Shatner comments and picked out a new mask for himself at the Haddonfield costume store. This was an empty vestige of the Dad I had known and loved. Gone was the glint in his eyes; they were instead dull and steely. That vacant expression was the most terrifying thing I had ever seen, but it wasn't something that I *had* ever seen.

Even on his deathbed, Dad hadn't allowed himself to budge an inch in his positivity, to cede any ground to defeat. And when he passed, when the light left his eyes, Dad's expression was serene and unbothered. *"Why am I remembering Dad like this? How can I imagine him looking anything like that? Why was he staring at me like that?"* I lost so many hours of sleep back then, I'm amazed that I was able to operate in any capacity, that I managed to do more than shuffle through my days like a partially-lobotomized zombie.

I felt such an overwhelming guilt: guilt over having lost my father in the first place, guilt over allowing myself, subconsciously or not, to recreate this ghastly version of him. I hoisted that compounded guilt up around my neck and shouldered it constantly. Where I was, there it was. The heaviness of that burden pressed down on me and filled my bones to bursting with an unrelenting ache, and I made not a sound in protest. When I moved, when I spoke, when I stirred, when I breathed, I felt it. I thought it would kill me, if I didn't kill myself first.

Chapter 13:
Ping Pong Show

"Yo, Z! Let's go!" Fuentes was banging on the door of my hotel room. Fuentes had boundless energy, he was peppy, he was zippy, he was flamboyantly heterosexual. He was also the best person to have as a travel buddy in Pattaya.

It was August; Kyle's funeral was in early May and I had been back to work in Hawaii for two months. My command sent me to train sailors in the Royal Thai Navy on equipment which, oddly enough, they didn't seem to possess. I made a personal vow to enjoy myself on what had basically amounted to a paid vacation to Thailand. I must have forgotten my promise to myself, then, because at that moment I was sprawled facedown on the bed, blackout curtains drawn fully closed, surrounded by empty candy wrappers and days-old room service trays. I guess I was enjoying myself a little bit, after all. "Come on, man! We're not sitting in the hotel the whole time we're here!"

I might have been cursing Fuentes under my breath, but I knew full well that I couldn't keep myself locked in that dark, cold room for another second. I hadn't left in three whole days, and my only company had been myself and the constant hum of the air conditioning unit, neither of which provided much in the way of riveting conversation. "This is fucking depressing," I muttered to myself. "Alright…just give me a second," I hoarsely shouted out to Fuentes. I hadn't spoken a single word in those three days, so the sound of my voice startled me.

I rolled onto my side with a great struggle, crumpling candy wrappers and scattering dirty silverware as I moved. I noticed that I had my shoes on. *"Why did I put my shoes on?"* The carpeting wasn't at all wet like it had been in India. *"Maybe I never took them off. One less thing I have to do, I guess."* I inched my way to the edge of the mattress and readied myself for the fall. I rocked backwards with what little energy I could muster, and then lurched forwards with a *thud* onto the dry yet stinky carpeted floor. A knife followed and hit me on the back of the head, thankfully with its handle and not its blade.

"Are you alright?! What's going on in there? Let me in!" Bless his sweet heart. I'd had my suspicions that our command leadership would be sending Fuentes along as some kind of suicide watch, and my suspicions were fully confirmed when I overheard Chief tell him "Make sure he doesn't kill himself, or I'll kill you." I didn't hold anything against him and I was glad he was chosen to accompany me, although I'm sure he spent his week of suicide patrol in a complete panic.

"I'm fine! I just…tripped." As if I'd managed to bring myself to my feet yet. I hadn't stood up in three days, either; the poor room service guys would come into the dark room, shriek when they thought they'd discovered a bloated corpse on the bed, and arrange the trays of food around me when they'd realize I was just fat and immobile. Next came the hard part; I wheezed as I brought myself to my hands and knees. I pictured an old, tired hippopotamus dragging itself out of the water and onto land, and I started laughing. I hadn't laughed in so long! The laughter inflated my lungs and propelled me upwards like a Garfield balloon in the Thanksgiving Day Parade.

My ankles cracked and my knees buckled; I was a little heavier than I was when I first flopped onto that bed. I stumbled across the room, shut off the air conditioner, and flung the curtains open, my muscles yelping in a startled fright from such a sudden and unexpected exertion of energy. The sunlight stung my eyes and burned my skin, and I raised a shriveled-up claw to cover my face like Nosferatu. When my eyes regained their vision, I looked down upon the sprawling beauty of Pattaya, spreading out like an enormous watercolor of the quintessential beachscape. The blue skies, white sands, green palms, neon pink and yellow beach blankets, boats with sails of every pastel hue imaginable: this brilliant rainbow erased every last trace of black in that hotel room and stirred in me just the tiniest sense of wonder. I wasn't well, but in that moment I could admit to feeling at least a close facsimile of "good."

"Z...?" Oh, Fuentes! I couldn't let him suffer a second longer. I unbolted the door and opened it for him, but not before spraying some air freshener to liven up that den of woe. It smelled like someone had thrown dead lilacs onto a pile of rotten leftovers, body odor, and farts.

"Hey, man..." his voice trailed off as he entered the room and started conducting a battle damage assessment. I should have at least thrown the comforter over my collection of dirty plates and empty ice cream cartons.

"Be right out!" I had darted into the bathroom before Fuentes could catch a glimpse of my inexplicably sunken yet bloated face. I splashed cold water on my face and greasy hair, applied a few coats of deodorant, and brushed my teeth, which really meant scraping away layers upon layers of yellow schmutz. I disgusted myself, which I interpreted as a good sign that my senses of dignity and shame were at least partially intact. Luckily, I had set my luggage down in the bathroom before entering hibernation, so Fuentes wouldn't see me in the same clothes I was wearing when we checked in. I don't know if he would have noticed something superficial like that, but I had and I was appalled. I gave myself a quick once-over in the mirror: clean clothes, washed face, scrubbed teeth, flat hair, defeated eyes, despondent expression. It all checked out! "So, where do you wanna go?"

"We're gonna go to the one place I just *know* you'll enjoy," Fuentes proudly promised as I emerged from the bathroom. His shoulders relaxed as he breathed a very audible sigh of relief. He looked me over as I had in the bathroom mirror just a moment earlier, scanning not my clothes but rather my face, my neck, my arms, my wrists.

"My bed?" I interrupted his survey. He shook his head no, but I was relieved that my sense of humor hadn't been smothered under an avalanche of Snickers, donuts, rocky road, and that funky Thai beer with an elephant riding a unicycle on the label.

"You'll see soon enough! It's a surprise!"

I exhaled sharply, not entirely up for an adventure into Thai parts unknown. Still, in the interest of not turning into a moss-covered sentient pile of dirt, I decided to humor my well-meaning shipmate. "Alright, let's go."

As we made our way through the crowded, sticky streets of Pattaya, my mind traveled back to India, back to the *damp*. Thailand was hot, too, but it didn't draw out the cataract of sweat quite as easily as India had. And whereas Goa smelled incredibly sweet, Pattaya had a rich, savory aroma hanging in the air over its produce stalls and souvenir carts. I thought of Putty, and I hoped she had eventually made it to that giant golden Buddha. I hoped, also, that she and her crew didn't resent me. "*I'm sorry my brother killed himself*," I thought to myself, and I realized immediately how ridiculous it sounded. Even Pushy, who'd threatened to shove me headfirst into an oven, must have felt bad, and hopefully reconsidered his proclivity for violence during emergency situations.

"*Thanks, Putty. I realize now that you knew about Kyle way before I did; that was a huge chunk of shitty knowledge to bear. Thanks for walking me through the hangar and keeping me company. I'm sorry you were kinda volunteered for that.*" Putty would find me on Facebook months later and share pictures of her trip to the Buddha, while I'd admit, to her amusement, to spending my time in Pattaya pursuing less wholesome activities.

"Well, here we are, Z!"

Fuentes had taken me to, of all places, Boyztown.

"Uh...Fuentes? You *do* realize what kind of place this is, don't you?" I asked over the electrical buzz of a neon "BOYS! BOYS! BOYS!" sign next to the entranceway to the alley.

"Yeah, man! I checked it out on Trip Advisor. This is like gay utopia!"

This wasn't so much a "gay utopia" as it was a place for married Western businessmen to satiate their piggish appetites without having to hide their wedding bands or think of a convincing explanation for those pesky tan lines on their ring fingers. But Fuentes had adorably searched "cool gay places in Pattaya" in an attempt to lift my spirits, so I went along with it. But first, a word of caution to Fuentes the Walking Hormone:

"Okay, Fuentes. You're going to come across some very sweet, very beautiful ladies in here. But these ladies aren't exactly…um…the kind of ladies that you might be used to. They're still ladies! Just…'different' ladies. Do you understand what I'm saying?"

"Relax, Z. I won't embarrass you in front of your people."

"*My people?*" Normally I'd launch into my soapbox lesson of how phrases like "*your people*" and "*those people*" are isolating in nature and stem from a mindset of operating in stereotypes, but I had just spent three full days withering away in a cave and I didn't have the energy. "Okay, as long as you're sure…"

"Yeah! Come on, it'll be fun!" I admired Fuentes' willingness to open himself up to a new experience, even if that experience was so far out of his comfort zone it might as well have been on another planet. "Lead the way." There was just a *smidge* of hesitation there after all, but I couldn't blame him.

I swung open the chain-link gate to Boyztown and heard Fuentes take a deep breath behind me. We had stepped into a veritable wonderland of neon signs, skittering strobe lights, and inches of glittery bare skin – which must have amounted to miles – everywhere the eye could see. And it was only ten thirty in the morning. Street food carts lined the skinny main thoroughfare, attracting crowds that packed the modest space and made maneuvering through feel like crowdsurfing while standing. An older white man wearing a fedora and a Hawaiian shirt yelled to us from a folding chair on the sidelines, "Put your wallets in your front pocket!" We did, and not a moment too soon: a shirtless kid pushed his way between me and Fuentes, his left hand rummaging through Fuentes' back pockets and his right hand through mine. He groaned in frustration when he realized someone had tipped us off to his little trick. Steep wooden steps scaled the tight spaces between parlors and day hotels. From what seemed like every open window, we heard cries of "Hello, American man!" and "You want lady boy?"

"Yo, Z, this is crazy!" Fuentes was grinning from ear to ear. "Look at that!" He pointed at a trio of go-go dancers in tiny shorts gyrating and twerking in a display window. A flashing sign above the window winked "ALL BOY ALL TIME" at us as we snaked our way through the crowd. We eventually came to a standstill; I felt fingers *everywhere* on my body, tickling, poking, and stroking. I sensed no real danger, but I was overwhelmed. I grabbed Fuentes by the wrist and we dove sideways, ducking into the nearest doorway.

"Hello," a gentle, unbothered voice called out from behind us. "You boys like ping pong show?"

We turned to see a wall of shimmering, sparkly beads. A vascular hand with an immaculate manicure thrust itself out from behind the beads, and drew them back halfway to reveal its tall, broad-shouldered, pretty owner. She slipped on a coy smile and turned her head down to look at us flirtatiously. She was a good six inches taller than either of us, so I have a hunch she did that so as not to look down upon and thus intimidate her customers; she traded on fragile Western masculinity, after all. "I'm call Miss Tran."

Miss Tran swept out from behind the shimmering wall and floated over to me and Fuentes. "Hmm? You like ping pong show?" she repeated in a husky whisper. She looked first at Fuentes, his grin somehow getting even wider and goofier, and then at me. I had learned months earlier what a ping pong show is, and my answer was a resounding *hell no*. "No…Not you," she said as she narrowed her eyes and studied my face. Miss Tran must have had a sixth sense. "But is okay. You friend watch, you have drink and relax."

"Uh…" I hoped, by this point, that Fuentes had figured out for himself what constitutes a ping pong show. "What's a ping pong show?" he asked in his enthusiastic, innocent way.

No such luck for me. Miss Tran and I exchanged a knowing glance and shared a chuckle. "Is better you no ask. Better you see,"

Miss Tran gripped us both by the shoulder with a strong hand and led us gingerly through the cascading wall of beads. Once inside, we saw a raised wooden stage framed on three sides by bleachers of about five rows. The bleachers were sparsely occupied by onlookers, most of whom were middle-aged men wearing rumpled business suits and dark sunglasses. Miss Tran yelled out a command in Thai in a tone much harsher than I could have imagined her summoning. She softened her face and chuckled gently when she saw me whip my head around in surprise. Two perfectly coiffed young ladies in bikini tops and denim short shorts appeared. One took my hand and the other Fuentes', and they led us in opposite directions.

"Uh...Z?" Fuentes sounded about as concerned as he could pretend to, being led by the hand by a beautiful, scantily-clad young lady who had obviously been instructed to treat him like royalty.

"It's all good, Fuentes! Just go along with it," I shouted supportively and gave him a thumbs up. I knew exactly what was about to go down, and I was sure it had started to dawn on Fuentes – based on the small audience of fidgety, raucous men – that a ping pong show is inherently sex-related.

The girl who had been assigned to keep me occupied smiled sweetly at me as we settled into our leather-cushioned stools at the bar. She barked an order in rapid Thai at the bartender, a scrawny boy who must have been no older than fourteen, and then swiveled her seat to observe my face. She had huge, expressive eyes which disclosed a mischievous spirit, and a funny little laugh to match. "Hi," she giggled and blushed. "My name Saengdao. What your name?"

"I'm Kevin. Nice to meet you...Sangdow?"

"No, not like 'Sangdow,'" she giggled and blushed even harder as she imitated my harsh American pronunciation. "Like 'Saengdao.'"

My untrained ears couldn't hear much of a difference between the two pronunciations, but I practiced saying "Saengdao" for five minutes before I managed to pronounce it to her satisfaction. "Is good, Kevin!" She pronounced my name more like "Kay-vayn," but it was adorable, so I allowed it. *"Close enough."* Our teenage bartender returned with two fishbowl-sized glasses, each filled with a sunrise in forty-four-ounce liquid form. Paper umbrellas and palm trees jutted out in a tangle, and plastic parrots were perched along the rims. Saengdao barked something else at the poor boy, sending him running in a tizzy to the other end of the bar. *"Damn, Saengdao. You sure can flip that switch in a hurry."*

I looked around to find where Fuentes had been herded. He was sitting front and center on the middle set of bleachers, and apparently had obtained VIP status since nobody else was sitting in the front row with him. His new friend, her arm draped around his neck, was touching his knee flirtatiously and giggling after every single thing he said; Fuentes is funny but not *that* funny. *"Please don't pay for sex, Fuentes."* The bleachers had filled in considerably since Miss Tran, strapping siren that she was, had lured us in. She was standing off to the side of the stage, smoking a cigar and surveying her haul, as girls scurried about behind her. The show was about to begin. *"I hope Fuentes can handle this."*

"Aw, you worry about you friend?" Saengdao asked, leaning her back against the bar and resting the fishbowl on the tops of her thighs. "You very sweet. No need worry."

"Oh, I know. I just…I don't think he understands what a ping pong show is."

"He find out soon enough!" Saengdao guffawed, sending a parrot flying off her glass. "You, uh…you 'funny man,' right?"

"Yeah, I'm a pretty funny guy," I replied, to Saengdao's visible disappointment; I had a feeling I knew exactly what she meant by "funny man." Still, I hoped that she would enjoy this opportunity to lean back, drink a comically large cocktail, and not be so concerned with laughing at my every word lest she incur the wrath of Miss Tran.

"Is too bad, but it happen," she conceded, and we proceeded to clink – or *clank,* in this case – our fishbowls to celebrate our new friendship. Fuentes was also drinking, but he was taking shots of what looked to be tequila with his new friend and a few rowdy businessmen who had tumbled out of their seats and into the front row. "You know, you have happy face. Even now, you not happy, but you face is."

"You can tell that I'm not happy?" These women had all kinds of auxiliary senses. Miss Tran could sense that I don't have a hankering for ping pong shows, and Saengdao could sense that I wasn't happy.

Saengdao nodded her head. "But is okay. No one always happy. Life sad sometime, life bad sometime. Life good again, sometime."

I looked her in the eye and smiled. "Thanks, Saengdao." My eyes got misty, but I refused to cry at a bar in Boyztown with a ping pong show setting up ten feet away from me.

"Oh, wow!" She was as proud of my pronunciation as a new mother hearing her baby utter a word with multiple syllables for the first time. "See? It get good!"

The bar lights flashed and a tinny-sounding song started blaring out of the speakers. That ditty may have been in Thai, but cheesiness transcends all language. Saengdao clicked her tongue and made an annoyed face at the speaker over our heads. The lights dimmed as the peal of a spotlight echoed throughout an otherwise hushed hall. "Showtime," she whispered.

A naked woman slid out from behind the curtain next to Miss Tran and sauntered onto the stage to obnoxious whoops and whistles from the audience. She was swinging a metal pail as she moved, and bent over dramatically to place it on the ground when she reached centerstage. I looked past her bare buttocks at Fuentes: his eyes were as big as saucers and his mouth hung open to his chest. "Look at you friend!" Saengdao laughed so hard that another parrot flew from its perch and she almost fell off her stool.

The star of the show assumed her position, sitting down on her bare behind with her feet flat on the stage, legs bent, and knees spread apart. She reached into her bucket and retrieved – you guessed it – a ping pong ball. By this point, Fuentes' jaw was on the floor and his eyes were bugging out of his head like Roger Rabbit. Now *I* was laughing; Saengdao and I leaned against each other in our shared fit of hysterics to keep from sliding onto the bar floor. I realized that I hadn't felt that happy, that blissfully detached from any and all negativity, in months.

"Thank you, Saengdao!" I wheezed through chortles and tears as a tiny *pop* triggered an uproar in that dingy Boyztown bar.

Chapter 14:
Coming Out

"Mom, Dad – I have something to tell you." I was fifteen and practicing in front of the bathroom mirror in a near whisper. I was on the brink of tears, I was trembling, I was scared shitless. But it was time to give voice to this thing. I had to hear it spoken out loud, to expel this truth from inside my head and cast it out into reality. It had become unbearable. "Please don't be mad at me, but...um...I hope you don't stop loving me. I'm still your son. Um...If I could change, I would. But I am...um...I think I might be gay. Please don't stop loving me."

I looked at myself in the mirror. I had greasy, pimply skin. I had a stupid little button nose that was so conspicuously not to the scale of my giant head. I was far too self-conscious to try and have a "cool" hairstyle, so my brown hair just sat there like a limp blob. "*It looks like poop.*" My eyebrows were starting to grow together and I hadn't even noticed. I wasn't tall, so there was no question as to which section Mom perused in the big and tall store where she shopped for me: I was fat. My clothes were baggy and always solid, dark colors; I refused to wear anything bright or with stripes that would attract any unnecessary attention to myself. I had a mouthful of braces and blue rubber bands. *"Why did I pick blue rubber bands? Why didn't I just go with the clear ones? Isn't it bad enough that I have to wear braces in the first place? Did I think they'd make me cool or 'different?' You don't need any help being different. You're such an idiot."* And those freckles! Those stupid, ugly freckles – they looked like splattered poop on my fat face. *"You're so ugly."* I was starting to think that it didn't even matter that I was gay; nobody would ever want anything to do with me in *that way*.

I wasn't very kind to myself. I loathed myself. I think I may have even been disgusted by myself. Yet, despite all the disdain I had thrown at my poor reflection in that bathroom mirror, at least a small part of me thought I was good enough to deliver a speech about my least favorite subject. Although I had yet to practice it outside of whispers in the bathroom, the time had come. I took a deep breath, unlocked the bathroom door, and stepped out into the upstairs hallway.

"Get out of the way, *faggot*," Kyle snarled at me as he stormed past, shoving me back into the bathroom. The door slammed shut and I slumped down onto the floor. I leaned my back against the tub, pulled my knees into my chest, and wrapped my arms tight around my legs. I was shell-shocked. Kyle had called me "queer," he had called me "gay," but he had never dropped the F-bomb on me. I heard him stomp down the stairs in his rage. The family photos that hung on the wall of the staircase shook and clattered.

"*What* is the problem?" Mom popped out of the kitchen, coffee pot in one hand and paper filters in the other; she was just about to start the afternoon coffee. Our family dog, Max, emerged behind her and whined nervously.

"Dad said I can't borrow the car!" Kyle screamed from the foot of the stairs, rattling the entire second story of our house.

"Kyle, you *totaled* his Ford Focus two weeks ago! Why are you at all surprised that he won't let you drive his new car?"

Kyle was unable to form a valid argument using human words, so he instead bellowed like an irate grizzly. Mom, unfazed as ever in the face of Kyle's fury, returned to her coffee. Max warily sniffed the air before following Mom.

"Calm down, Son." Dad had followed Kyle down the stairs and was now trying to inject a modicum of serenity into the atmosphere.

"This is *bullshit!*" Dad's call for peace had fallen on deaf ears. The storm blew past him and whipped circles around the dining room table, dangerously close to the living room where Kelly was napping. Emphasis on *was*. My sister usually has a fairly pleasant disposition, but if one does something foolish like wake her from a nap or scream in her face, Beast makes an appearance faster than

Edward Hyde can rip out of Dr. Jekyll to trample hapless villagers. Kyle had already committed one of those egregious trespasses, and his blind fury would soon send him careening into the heart of hostile territory.

"What's going on out here?" Kelly stumbled out of her slumber, pillow creases lining her face. She had arrived just that morning on leave, this time from Rota, Spain, and was exhausted.

"It's none of your goddamn business!" Kyle screamed at Kelly, squaring up against her from across the dining room.

Kelly didn't say a word. She pulled her bob back into a tight little nub and cracked her knuckles. If she had been wearing earrings, she'd take them off; if she'd had a jar of Vaseline handy, she'd be greasing up her face. She was *ready*.

"Oh boy." Dad escaped to the safety of the kitchen, where Mom had a cup of coffee waiting for him. "Should we do something?"

"Are you crazy?" Mom scoffed. "Kelly's never here; let her deal with him." She pulled a few pages out of the newspaper, opened in front of her on the kitchen table, and handed them to Dad. "Read your sports section."

Dad didn't protest. "Let's see how my stupid Knicks are doing," he complied, taking the paper from Mom and happily taking a seat at the table. Max rested his head on Dad's feet.

Meanwhile, I had slumped onto the middle landing of the staircase for a ringside seat to *Kelly vs. Kyle: The Rematch*. My feelings were so deeply hurt: not only did Kyle call me a word that *Anthony* had once wielded against me – one I had hoped my own flesh and blood would be above using – but my siblings' boisterous antics on that evening would most assuredly drown out anything at all that I had to say. I resigned myself to sitting on the sidelines with my hurt feelings, staying clear of the skirmish.

"You know," Kelly said in her unbothered, matter-of-fact way, "You're a real asshole."

"What the fuck do *you* know?" Kyle shot back.

"I *know*," she volleyed back across the court, "That the last time you acted like a little prick, I kicked your ass and your braces ended up stuck in the carpet."

"*Watch out, Kelly,*" I thought to myself. Kyle wasn't the same troublemaking little scamp from two years prior. He was at least a foot taller than her, at least forty pounds heavier than her, and was no longer encumbered by a mouthful of metal. He had also honed his temper into a terrifying aggression that would make Michael Myers cancel his Halloween plans and maybe try again next year.

"*Fuck you.*" There wasn't the tiniest bit of levity in Kyle's voice. He was livid about having been denied driving privileges, and had found a suitable proxy for his ire. It if hadn't been Kelly, it would've been me. All I could do was offer her my sincerest gratitude in complete silence.

"You can't just scream like a maniac when you don't get your way. If you don't settle down on your own, I'll *make* you settle down," Kelly promised sternly, without a trace of fear in *her* voice.

"Wow. She'll be a great parent one day," Dad would later recall proudly telling Mom, as the two of them raised a cup of coffee to their daughter and her eventual parenting prowess.

"*You* don't get to tell me what to do. Go back to Italy, or wherever the fuck you live now."

"Okay, just get this over with already," I grumbled to myself, but not too loud, lest Kyle remember there was a much bigger, much slower target just up the stairs. My cat Bobby, about as fat as I was, had waddled down the stairs and settled in my lap. He, too, was growing impatient waiting for Zalinsky Deathmatch '02. We wouldn't have to wait long, however, because…

Kyle called Kelly the "C" Word.

Without hesitation, Kelly leapt through the air in a recreation of her infamous move from the Braces Incident. She wasn't able to send Kyle hurtling to the ground like back then, so she wrapped her limbs around him like a spider monkey squeezing open a coconut. Kelly had again stunned him with her impossible quickness, but Kyle managed to dislodge her and send her flying across the dining room. Kelly crashed into the dining room table, toppling two heavy wooden chairs upon impact.

"You don't use *that word*, you asshole!" she screamed upon regaining her balance after propelling herself off the side of the table. Kelly's offense at his use of the "C" Word matched Kyle's own indignation at the denial of his request to drive Dad's new used car. It was getting *intense*; Bobby and I scooted down four more steps to get a closer look at the action. I remember hearing the kitchen radio getting louder as the brawl intensified.

Kelly reached down to hoist up a chair. "*Is she going to hit him with that?!*" I exclaimed to myself, craning my head out of the staircase and around the wall of the dining room. It was heavier than she had anticipated; she managed to lift it only a few inches off the ground before dropping it with a *thud*. Kyle took advantage of her fumble and charged at her, wrapping his arms around her waist and tackling her backwards into the living room. Kelly shrieked like a banshee and dug both her heels into the floor and her fingernails into Kyle's face, to little avail.

The pair of them, entangled in a ball of flailing limbs like one of those old-school cartoon fight clouds, collided with the back of the plaid living room couch. First, Kyle slammed Kelly against the couch; Kelly then used every ounce of her strength to swap places with Kyle and slam *him* against the couch. They took turns beating up on our poor couch with one another until it teetered onto its disproportionately tiny wooden legs and flipped over entirely, trapping my brother and sister underneath. By this point, Mom and Dad could no longer feign ignorance and relax in the relative serenity of the kitchen.

"Alright, alright! Break it up, you two!" Dad very, very rarely raised his voice, but he could no longer abide this ridiculous rumble. Max ran from one end of the couch to the other, growling and barking at the raucous brawlers in an attempt to break them up.

"My couch! Damn it!" Mom is actually the originator of the phrase "this is why we don't have nice things." She'd scream it the *next* time her couch played a pivotal role in a bout between two of her kids; it would unfortunately not survive that encounter. In *this* instance, however, it provided Kelly just the right amount of support needed to brace her feet against one of its upside-down armrests and press Kyle's head against the other. She dug her fingers into his neck until his head looked like a tomato mere seconds from exploding.

"Ow!" Kelly yelped and released her claws from Kyle's neck. Max had squeezed his head under the overturned couch and proceeded to bite her on the ass. Dad seized the opportunity afforded by this unintentional ceasefire and flipped the couch right-side up. He pulled Kyle in one direction as Mom pulled Kelly in the other.

"That's enough!" Mom announced. Kelly and Kyle were both doubled over and panting, much too drained to continue their war of attrition. At least neither of them wound up with a bloody nose or attached to the carpet. "Kelly, go to the kitchen; I made coffee. Kyle, go…somewhere. You can use the car again when you're not acting like a lunatic. And we ordered Chinese food while you two were killing each other."

With the bout called in a draw, Kelly dragged herself into the kitchen to nurse her wounds. Kyle, however, hadn't yet scratched the fighting itch to his full satisfaction. He stormed onto the enclosed front porch and kicked out an entire window with one strike of his bare foot. The Chinese food delivery man, whose finger just so happened to be approaching the doorbell at that exact moment, dropped the cardboard box containing our food onto the stoop. "Oh! Oh!" he yipped at the sight of Kyle's foot crashing through the window in a torrent of shattered glass. Kyle ripped past him and disappeared into the garage, where he'd stew in his anger for a few hours.

"How much do I owe you?" Dad appeared with an open wallet, all too eager to pay the frazzled man and send him on his merry way.

"Th-th-thirty-two…f-fifty," the bewildered man stammered. Dad gave him forty, waved at him as he peeled out of the driveway in reverse, and scooped up our order which had miraculously remained intact. "The won ton soup didn't spill," he noted in wonder as he handed the box off to Mom. "I'll clean up this mess; you and the kids eat." Just a typical family dinner in the Zalinsky household!

"Kids, dinnertime!" Mom was halfway through the dining room when she heard me sniffling on the stairs. "Kelly, take this into the kitchen." My sister obliged, taking the box of food from Mom. I could see the comingled looks of guilt and concern on my sister's face as she strained to find me in the shadows of the staircase. Mom tapped her on the shoulder, lightly shooing her into the kitchen to give me my privacy.

"Hi, Honey. What's the matter?" Mom stood at the foot of the stairs, resting her forearm on the bannister as she leaned in to get a closer look at me. Bobby and I had scooched back onto the safety of the landing. I was busying myself with petting the cat; he was purring loudly and totally submerged in bliss.

"Thanks for keeping Bobby out of that warzone," Mom chuckled. She walked up the stairs and plopped down next to me. "Your brother and sister are crazy," she sighed.

"Yep."

"And thank you for being such a good kid." Mom wrapped her arm around my neck and pulled me in to kiss my cheek.

"Uh-huh."

"You should have seen the poor Chinese delivery man! Your brother scared him half to death. Don't worry, though – the food is fine."

"Great."

"We ordered your favorite – sweet and sour chicken! Why don't we go eat it while your brother's off God-knows-where? He doesn't need to know that we got any."

"…Okay."

"Okay! Let's go, Honey." I moved Bobby out of my lap and Mom and I stood up together. She kept her arm wrapped around my shoulders as we walked down the stairs and into the kitchen, and gave one tight squeeze before letting me go. "Alright, let's eat! Kelly, I'm sure you worked up quite an appetite!"

As we pulled the paper cartons out of the cardboard box, assessing the damage and arranging them on the kitchen counter, we heard Dad sweeping up the glass on the front porch and whistling *Bad Moon Rising*. He waved at our next-door neighbor, Frank, who was standing in his front lawn and probably figuring out whether or not he had to call 911. "Nice night, huh?" Dad asked, and Frank resumed his nightly routine of drinking beer and watching the scrambled dirty channels in his garage. His nosey wife peeked through her kitchen blinds at Mom, who had a less neighborly hand gesture to offer. Mrs. Frank pulled her fingers out of the blinds and probably proceeded to call the other neighbors to complain about "those people" – my family.

"Phew, alright." Dad joined us after a few minutes as we were plating. "Well, I guess we can't order from Golden China II ever again," he sighed.

"It's a shame – their won ton soup is the best," Mom lamented as she poured herself a bowlful.

"How many places have blacklisted us because of Kyle?" Kelly asked with great concern. My sister is the biggest foodie of us all; she'd have come home on leave even less if the number was too great.

"Oh, just one pizza place," Mom replied. "What did he do to them, again?"

"He was chasing Kevin outside and he slammed the screen door into the poor delivery guy," Dad reminded her.

"Was the pizza ruined?" Kelly asked, with even greater concern.

"The cheese got shifted around a little, but it was fine. They were overreacting, if you ask me."

"Come on; let's eat, Son. Your mom and I ordered your favorite."

I had a very specific goal in mind at the outset of that evening. I had it all figured out. I ran through the scenario over and over in my mind, and every time it went the same way: perfectly. *"Tonight is the night that I come out to Mom, Dad, Kelly...and I guess Kyle again if he's around. By the end of this night, they're going to know a little bit more about me, but they aren't going to love me any less."* Kelly would pull me close and call me her "brave baby brother." Mom would cry, but only because "her Honey" had revealed more of himself and allowed her further into his life. Dad would tear up, too, and then grip me in a tight hug and say, "I'll always love you, Son." "Told you so," Kyle would playfully gloat before promising me, "We're with you no matter what, Kev."

That's not how things went for me. I had envisioned my brother celebrating my revelation and praising my newfound courage; he instead hurled *the* slur at me and threw an epic temper tantrum over not getting to borrow Dad's car. My sister, rather than being the bigger person and superior Taurus, chose not to leave well enough alone but instead to gleefully goad the bull with her red cape. My meager confidence was trampled in the ensuing mayhem. But that's not to say that the blame rests squarely on my siblings' shoulders: I kicked the night off by listing all the things I hated about myself, only to retreat deeper into my negative headspace as the house was torn apart around me. But, looking back with a couple decades' worth of perspective, I'm so very proud of myself. *"You're still here. All those terrible things you thought about yourself, that disdain you built up as you bullied your own reflection, the disgust that sat like a brick in your stomach as you looked in the mirror, and you're still here. Thank you."*

Chapter 15:
The Other "C" Word

"Son of a *bitch*!"

Mom has a voice that could probably shatter glass if she were to scream loud enough. I swear I heard the windows crackle on this particular occasion. Kyle and I were sitting at the dining room table. It was a Sunday afternoon, I was sixteen, he was on the edge of nineteen, and we were studying for his final exams. Some kind-hearted, clueless stranger might come upon us and think "How nice of this young man to help his older brother study!" but my well of altruism was actually quite shallow. If Kyle didn't pass these exams, he wouldn't graduate from high school, which meant that he'd have to repeat his senior year, which meant that I would be stuck with him for an additional 365 days. So, I stayed up all night making hundreds of flashcards without a single complaint, and we hunkered down for the weekend with four family-size bags of Cheetos and a case of Red Bull.

"What did you do?" I whispered across the table at Kyle.

"I don't think I did anything. I've been home all weekend."

"Oh, yeah…" It hadn't dawned on me until I heard it spoken out loud: *Kyle had been home all weekend.* Usually, Kyle would be gone from three p.m. on Friday until ten p.m. on Sunday, with a quick call to Mom and Dad on Saturday evening so they wouldn't panic and assume he was dead. He must have really been taking these exams seriously if he cleared his social calendar *and* community mischief schedule in order to study at home with me.

"Okay, what's on the next card?"

"What is…the 'representativeness heuristic?'" I asked, trying not to let my face droop into a presumptive expression of pity.

"Well!" Mom announced her presence and the windows crackled a little more. "I went through yesterday's mail and found something very interesting!"

"It's a strategy of figuring something out based on what you already know, or assume you already know, instead of wasting time by looking up all the facts," Kyle answered to a pleasantly surprised me. "What's up, Mom?"

"We got our wedding invitation to your cousin Reggie's wedding." Mom didn't deliver this presumably good news with any of her usual pep.

"Oh, cool," Kyle mumbled as he looked for "representativeness heuristic" on his list of psychology terms and crossed it off. "When is it, again? I'll make sure we don't book any gigs."

Dad shuffled into the dining room and took a seat opposite me, next to Kyle. He put his elbow on the table and rested his head in the palm of his hand. He looked at Mom knowingly.

"It's sometime in July," Mom answered, pulling out the chair next to me. "But we're not going."

"What? But we were talking about it the whole time in Key West!" We had returned from Florida, and our decennial McCormick-Hagan family reunion, two weeks prior. If *one* loud, rowdy, drunken Irish family descending upon a quiet beach town just screams "fun for us, headaches for everybody else," can you imagine what *two* would scream? It *was* a lot of fun, though.

Mom and Dad exchanged a glance as she handed the invitation to Kyle. "Reggie and Patricia cordially blah blah blah in the union of two blah blah on July whenever at the old whatever in blah blah blah…John and Kathy Zalinsky? Where are me and Kevin? I don't see our names."

"We're not invited," I deduced. I wasn't too crestfallen; my cousin Reggie is ten years older than me, and we didn't have very much in common when I was a teenager. He and Kyle were always able to talk about baseball and pre-Civil War history, two of Kyle's favorite nonsexual topics of discussion.

"No way! We're family – of course we're invited! They probably just ran out of space. Look at all the flowers and shit on this thing," Kyle explained as he waved the tacky invitation around.

"No, Honey." Mom clasped her hands in front of her on the table. "I called your Aunt Veronica and asked her, and she told me only 'contemporary cousins' are invited to the wedding."

"Contemporary cousins?" Kyle asked as he flung the invitation onto the table. "What the hell are contemporary cousins?"

"I think it means cousins that are close to the same age?" I shrugged, not entirely buying that line of bullshit.

"It's bullshit," Mom said, vindicating my doubts. "You *are* a contemporary cousin!" she vehemently informed Kyle before glancing over at me and asking, "You don't really care, do you?"

I shook my head no. I couldn't care less, but I *did* feel bad for my brother. In Florida, he'd hang out with Reggie and all of our other older cousins all day, and then drink them under the table at the resort tiki bar every night. (Remember: this was a dual Irish family reunion.)

"Don't feel bad, Son." Dad lightly tapped Kyle on the chin with his fist. "It's not personal; weddings are expensive."

"Man…this sucks." Kyle dropped his hands into his lap and slumped back in his chair. I don't think I'd ever seen him so deflated. "You guys gotta go!" He shook his head, along with the look of disappointment from his face, and snapped himself out of his funk.

"We're not going if our kids aren't invited!" Mom grabbed my hand and extended her other for Kyle to take. He shook his head again.

"No way. Everyone else is gonna be there. It'll be fun. I want you guys to go and have a good time. Dad deserves to—" Kyle cut himself off. His gaze shifted immediately away from the table and his eyes glazed over. Dad rested his hand on the back of Kyle's neck.

"Don't worry about me, Son. There will be lots of other weddings that we can all go to – *together.*" Kyle nodded his head, still avoiding eye contact. He didn't seem fully convinced.

"That's right! Like when *you* get married!" Mom chirped and gestured at Kyle. "And maybe we just won't invite th—"

"Kathy…" Dad took her hand which Kyle had refused and cut Mom off, softly and with great caution. Mom doesn't generally take too kindly to being interrupted, but she uncharacteristically obliged in this instance. She gave Dad a slight smile and squeezed his hand. "I'm gonna go lie down in the den. Kyle, don't let this bother you too much, okay?"

Dad let go of Mom's hand and pushed his chair out with a groan. He pressed his elbows down into the table and thrust himself up onto his feet. He put his hands on my brother's shoulders and shook him playfully before shuffling out of the dining room. Kyle's eyes had become watery; he was now biting down on his lip.

"His treatments are going well," Mom whispered to us after we heard the door to the den close. "It would've been nice to go to this wedding, but your dad is going to get thr—" Kyle pushed his chair out from the dining room table, causing his stack of memorized index cards to topple. He stormed out of the dining room, and Mom and I followed his heavy footsteps up the stairs to his bedroom. He slammed the door behind him and stayed in his room for the rest of the afternoon.

* * *

"Alright, Son. Let's go see Dr. Finklefinger!" Dad's proctologist was named Dr. Finklestein, and Dad, never having fully outgrown the bawdy sense of humor of a United States Marine, instead called him "Dr. Finklefinger." He wagged his index finger in my face.

"Dad…Gross!" I groaned as I pulled my face away from Dad and his wriggling finger.

"Don't be late for Dr. Finklestein!" Mom yelled up from the laundry room in the basement.

"We're leaving right now!" I yelled back down.

Every Friday afternoon, much like Sunday mornings when I was a kid, Dad and I had our routine: I'd come straight home from school and assemble his smorgasbord of medicine; he'd get home from work at two thirty on the dot and meet me in the kitchen, where he'd wash down his pills with a shot of prune juice; and we'd attempt to make it out the front door before Mom had a chance to yell "Don't be late for Dr. Finklestein!" from the laundry room.

I wrapped my arm around Dad's pointy elbow and pulled him close to me. His arm was bonier than I could ever recall it being, but I wasn't too alarmed; not then, anyway. We shuffled slowly out to his car, which had become the tipping point for the infamous Couch Incident, and I eased Dad down into the front seat. Being the economical family that we are, these trips doubled as check-ups with Dr. Finklefinger for Dad and driving lessons for me.

"Remember to adjust your side-view mirrors before taking off, Son." Lessons with Dad were a relaxing exercise in building up my confidence and quelling any fears I may have had of driving on chaotic New Jersey roads. Lessons with Mom were more like driving the bus from *Speed*, except I couldn't drive below ninety miles per hour and the bus was on fire and filled with yowling cats which were also on fire.

"Got it, Dad. You ready?" He'd squeeze my right forearm as confirmation and we'd be off.

"There's my favorite patient!" Dr. Finklefinger would practically swoon every time Dad walked into the waiting room of his office.

"Hi, Johnny," the receptionist would coo from behind her desk and wiggle her fingers in a dainty little wave.

"Tell me, Kevin, have you been taking good care of your dad?" Dr. Finklefinger shook Dad's hand with one hand and gripped his shoulder with the other.

Dad smiled and nodded. "He's the best one I've got, taking his dad every week to get his rear end fingered."

"Dad!" I gasped in mortified embarrassment as the doctor guffawed and his receptionist tittered.

"Alright! Well, let's get a finger in there," Dr. Finklefinger led Dad back to the exam room as I tried not to violently implode and collapse in on myself.

Dad was back there for longer than usual that day. He would, to my absolute horror, describe the typical process to me as follows: "I strip down, I get a little poke, I pull my pants back on, I leave the money on the side table, and I get kicked out."

"All good?" I asked when Dad emerged from the back. Dr. Finklefinger gave him a hug and a hearty pat on the back before waving goodbye to me.

"All good," he said. "Let's go home, Son."

"Bye, Johnny!" the receptionist called out as the front door closed behind us.

Dad would usually take a nap on the ride home, and that afternoon was no exception. His nodding off would say to me that he had complete confidence in my driving ability; I'm probably reading too much into it, but that's my theory and I'm standing by it. Dad jolted awake as we pulled into the driveway. "Home sweet home," he mumbled in a groggy voice. Normally, after an appointment with Dr. Finklefinger, Dad would ask me to take him to directly to his recliner in the den, where he'd doze off for the hour or so before dinner. Not this time.

"Kathy!" Dad called out as soon as we stepped through the front door. Mom, busy making coffee as on most afternoons, popped her head out of the kitchen. "Can we talk, Dear?" Her happy expression faded almost instantly. After twenty-six years of marriage, Mom and Dad had come to intimately understand every minor inflection and subtle discrepancy in tone. "Thanks, Son." Dad affectionately patted me on the head as Mom slid her arm around his waist and led him into the kitchen. I went upstairs to play video games; I was oblivious.

I wish I had paused then, for even a measly second, to catch a glimpse of Mom and Dad – her arm wrapped tightly around him, his head resting gently on the top of hers – framed by the kitchen doorway like some forgotten cover of *The Saturday Evening Post*. Dad received bad news at that afternoon's appointment: news so bad that no amount of "Dr. Finklefinger" jokes could soften its blow; news so bad that sweet little snapshots like that one – fleeting moments one doesn't usually bother committing to memory – became all too rare in our home.

"The cancer has metastasized." I had no idea what that phrase meant, but I'd overhear Mom whisper it into the cordless home phone a lot that following week. Well, Mom is physically incapable of whispering, so I didn't have to develop too sophisticated of an eavesdropping training regimen. Whatever that word was, it wasn't "gone" or "cured" or "remission," so I knew it couldn't be good. I guess I could have consulted a dictionary or whatever crude version of WebMD was knocking around our dial-up Internet at the time, but I just couldn't bring myself to do it. Instead, I'd slump down onto the floor outside Mom and Dad's closed bedroom door, and I'd listen for the essential elements of information.

In times of crisis as in times of jubilation, Mom has a very specific phoning order. First up: her only sister, my Aunt Margie. Second is Uncle Mike, the oldest and therefore wisest of Mom's brothers, followed by Uncles Jake, Rick, and baby brother Dale. Mom said the same thing to all of her siblings: "The cancer has metastasized." She didn't burst into tears, nor did her voice did quake when she delivered the news; she maintained a calm, even tone, which led me to believe that we hadn't passed the panic threshold just yet.

"Dad is fine. He's absolutely fine. He takes his medicine, he drinks his prune juice, he sees Dr. Finklefinger, Mom stays on top of everything...Once he cuts back on his hours at work, everything will be better. He just has to slow down a little, that's all. If things were

bad, Mom and Dad would tell us; they tell us everything. Things are fine."

"Kevin, are you still out there? Come in here, Honey."

Chapter 16:
Zombie

The darkest hour of my life was actually thirteen hours. I was on an overnight flight from Tokyo to New York's LaGuardia Airport. The plane was so sparsely occupied, I can remember seeing only two other people: a flight attendant, and a man three rows in front of me who asked the flight attendant if he could move away from me – my sobbing and heaving must have been annoying. That flight attendant would end up checking on me a grand total of one time during the entire flight, when we were about to land and she had to ask me, in broken English, to return my tray table to the upright position. Sheets of paper in various stages of distress were strewn across the table and both empty seats next to mine. Normally, I guess one would take advantage of having the entire row to oneself and spread out, maybe even get a few hours' sleep. I, however, had no such luxury: I had a eulogy to write.

I had never felt so alone in my entire life. I'm someone who treasures his alone time; solitary confinement has never seemed like much of a punishment to me. Even so, those thirteen hours were unbearable. I'd look around, and see only the tops of a few heads in the very front of the plane. Perhaps I was in solitary confinement and I hadn't even realized it. I can imagine the flight crew being directed to keep the crazy, hysterical American in seclusion at the back of the plane, and away from the other passengers who were unlucky enough to draw a series of short straws and end up on that flight. I'd open the plastic shade to look for any signs of life on the other side of the window – pitch black. Even the moon and stars had hidden themselves away from me. Maybe they, too, were mourning.

I didn't know how I was going to write Kyle's eulogy, but I did know that I'd have to figure something out. Mom would be far too distraught, and Kelly has never handled emotions, especially the icky ones, very well. *"What am I supposed to write? I'm not qualified to say a goddamn word about you, Kyle. Shit.*" I figured, if I couldn't find within myself the right words to convey just who Kyle was and the way he charged through life with total abandon, I could look to his idols for inspiration. I would never admit it to him, but it wasn't just bruises that I'd collected from Kyle over the years: every so often, a song – "Come Together" or "Lola" or "Tumbling Dice" or "I Can See for Miles" – would come blaring out of his stereo and grab me by the ear.

I'd write down any lyrics I could make out between our two closed bedroom doors and the hallway which separated them, and ask Mom and Dad at the breakfast table the following morning if they could identify the source. "Sure, Honey, that's…*Prudence*! Right, John?" "*Dear Prudence*, Dear." I took my iPod out of my carry-on. I was relieved I'd had the foresight to throw it into my backpack and not a random piece of checked luggage. There were four bags in the belly of that plane with my name on them; I was supposed to spend six months in Japan, and I managed to get through four and a half.

The iPod battery was at forty percent. "*Shit. I must have put the charger in a different bag. Just get this over with, Kevin.*" My eyes were bloated with tears and heavy from exhaustion. As soon as my commanding officer had broken the news to me, and Kendall somehow managed to hoist me onto my feet, I was off: first, back to my barracks room to pack up all my belongings in the dark as my roommate tossed, turned, and sighed heavily because I was disrupting his beauty sleep; then, into the duty van for the hour-long trip from Yokosuka to Tokyo. Another selfless friend of mine, Joanna, had volunteered to accompany me on this ride. She wrapped her arm around my shoulders for that entire hour and never once let me go, no matter how hard I sobbed, shuddered, or heaved. I will never forget her kindness, although I'm sure I was unable to articulate my gratitude at the time.

First up in the rotation was Sir Paul McCartney. I was reminded how, rather tellingly, Paul was my favorite Beatle and John was Kyle's. I've always drawn a parallel between their sometimes okay, mostly tumultuous relationship and our own. Kyle was the John to my Paul; it's so funny, describing the two of us with apostolic names. I pulled out a handful of random papers that I had shoved into my backpack in my great hurry to leave, found a ballpoint pen knocking around in the seatback pouch in front of me, and pressed "shuffle" on my Paul playlist.

Fine Line kicked things off. *"Okay...It's a little corny, and more than a little vague...Not sure if I can use this one."* And then I was punched in the gut. Paul sang, in a voice heavy with years of caked-on regret, something about forgiving his brother, crying when he left, and begging him to come back home. My chest heaved as I gasped for air between sobs. If I were that other passenger, I would've demanded a seat as far away as possible from the gasping lunatic, too. I tried to lay my head down on the tray table; it didn't fit. Instead, I plopped down onto my side and used the stack of assorted papers as a very sad pillow. *"I'm only on the first song. I'll never get through this."*

But I had to get through it. It was the least I could do for Kyle. It was also the last thing I'd be able to do for him. *"Damn it."* I dragged myself upright using the seatbacks of the row in front of me, and I moved onto the next Beatle. Surely George, that gentle, enlightened soul who floated above the petty drama and base squabbling, wouldn't break my heart? Well, he proved to be no better than the rest of the Fab Four, because *What is Life* played and he proceeded to break my fucking heart. *"Thanks, George! Next up: Ringo. Peppy Ringo Fucking Starr couldn't possibly make me feel any sadder."* I played *Photograph* – the sole Ringo song on my iPod – and was immediately reminded of just how depressing it is. Delete. *"You had one chance and you blew it, Ringo."*

I yanked the earbuds out of my head, pulled myself to my feet, and sidled out into the very narrow aisle meant for thin Japanese passengers and not an American engorged by fatigue and despair. I braced myself against the seats on either side of the aisle. The flight attendant was peeking at me from behind the curtains she had pulled shut to separate me from the humans in the front of the plane. Don't contaminated animals get water, at the very least, when they're in quarantine? "Eek!" I heard her yelp in fear and scurry away. *"I'll get my own water, arigato."*

When I squeezed myself into the tiny bathroom for quarantined creatures at the rear of the plane and the harsh yellow light flickered on, I was distraught when I saw my reflection in the mirror. I barely recognized myself. I had gotten into great shape during my four months in Japan, but my face reflected exactly none of that hard-won health. My cheeks were sunken in and caked with dried-on tears. My eyes had passed over "bloodshot" and opted instead for the "malfunctioning laser-eyed robot" look.

My lips were gray and cracked; I couldn't find my lip balm and salty tears had proven to be a poor substitute. My skin, anemic and draped loosely over my cheekbones, was practically sliding off my face. I had managed to perfect the shambling corpse look, no prosthetics or Halloween makeup necessary. I filled the miniature sink with cold water, scooped it up with both hands, and doused my haggard face. I could barely feel the cold; I had become so very numb. I didn't even bother to dry my face off before shuffling back through the empty cabin to my seat. The scattered, tear-stained papers helped me pick out my row from the countless vacant others. *"Alright, Johnny boy. Let's get this over with."*

John Lennon was Kyle's personal hero. I think my brother saw more than a little of himself in John: conflicted, misunderstood, passionate, deeply sensitive underneath the posturing. I've never allowed myself to relate to John Lennon, to feel anything when I hear any part of his undeniably stellar catalog. I will forever link my brother to his personal hero, and I can't listen to "#9 Dream" or "Woman" or "Instant Karma!" or "Imagine" without, yes, *imagining* Kyle, singing along and teaching himself the guitar chords. That inextricable connection is probably why I had – and have – a handful of John Lennon's songs on my iPod. Not for my personal enjoyment, but as a small digital shrine to Kyle. With great hesitation, I clicked on his name and shuffled the playlist of eight songs. *"Is Kyle watching the wheels go 'round with you, John?"*

* * *

145

"Do you want some banana bread, Kev?"

"I made banana bread, Sweetie. Here, I cut you a slice."

"Your Aunt Margie made banana bread. Have a piece, Honey."

I was buried under an avalanche of banana bread the second I opened the front door to Aunt Margie and Uncle Tim's house. Three paper plates spilling over with the stuff were thrust in my face before I could even set my backpack on the floor. In my family, we drink our feelings; when drinking is deemed not the most appropriate coping mechanism for that particular scenario, we then eat our feelings. My cousin Pete dragged two of my checked bags through the front door behind me. He had picked me up from the airport and warned me that there would be banana bread.

"Oh no, I'm not very hungry." Pete took me through the White Castle drive-thru before bringing me to his parents' house. "Thank you, though."

"Oh, Honey!" Mom dropped her paper plate onto the coffee table and hugged me as if she hadn't seen me in decades. When she pulled away, I was able to take an up-close gander at her face; the undead family resemblance was uncanny. "Oh, my God, you look terrible!" she laughed, sniffling her nose and wiping away the top layer of tears with the back of her hand.

"Gee, thanks." I snorted and felt my nose discharge *something* down the front of my face.

"Here's a tissue, Sweetheart!" Aunt Margie pulled a balled-up tissue out of the pocket of her cardigan and reached towards my face. I blocked her hand as politely as is possible when one squashes the tender affections of a loved one, and took the tissue from her. No matter how distraught I might have been, I wasn't about to let my saintly aunt clean my snotty face.

"Thanks, Aunt Margie." The tissue attached itself to my face via either boogers or dirt. I hadn't showered since…"What day is it?"

Mom looked at Aunt Margie. Aunt Margie looked at Uncle Tim. Uncle Tim looked at Pete. Pete looked at his phone. "It's Tuesday."

"Holy shit," Mom sighed. "The funeral's on Thursday." She pulled herself back against me and buried her face in my shirt. I hadn't felt an emotion in hours, but now my heart ached more and more with each subsequent Mom sob until I thought it would just quit. "Jesus, Kevin! What is this shit all over your shirt?" Mom reared her head back in disgust and started laughing through the deluge of tears.

"What?" I asked in a high-pitched affronted voice. "I haven't changed my clothes since India! It's just food. Oh, wait…I haven't eaten since India. It's just boogers."

"Oh, my God," Mom was laughing so hard she started to cry. Well, she had been crying since Sunday morning, but now at least a small portion of the tears slathered across her face had humor to blame. If we can't drown our pain or smother it with food, we find something – *anything* – to laugh at so we can ignore it, even for a few seconds. Mom and I pointed at my boogery shirt and doubled over while Margie, Tim, and Pete looked at us like we had cracked beyond repair.

"What's going on?! I heard Mom crying from the street!" Kelly came hurtling through the front door, plastic shopping bags swinging wildly as if they'd been snagged by a tornado. "Kevin!"

"Hi, Kelly." I got ahold of myself and gave my sister a big hug. Her hair was pulled into a loose ponytail and didn't have its usual sheen; she wore baggy sweatpants and the oversized Navy sweatshirt she's had since boot camp; her eyes were red-rimmed from crying or exhaustion or both. She wouldn't be admiring herself in the mirror anytime soon.

"I'm so glad you're home. Thanks for picking him up, Pete. How was—"

"Did you get my coffee?" Mom broke up our reunion to get a closer look at the groceries. Aunt Margie and Uncle Tim don't usually drink coffee, so I'm sure they didn't get the "right kind" for Mom, and the funeral preparations had kept her from going to the store herself.

"Folgers!" Kelly pulled a giant red can out of one of the bags to assuage Mom's anxiety. Mom snatched it from her and ran into the kitchen as Pete and Uncle Tim unhooked the other groceries from my sister's arms. "So how was your flight?"

"Jesus. Where do I start?" I plopped down on the living room sofa and cradled my head in my hands. Kelly sat down next to me and wrapped me in a side hug. "It was rough."

"I'm so sorry that you found out that way." Kelly was the one who had been in regular contact with the Red Cross, and they designated her to be the familial bearer of bad news. I spoke to her very briefly on my commanding officer's office phone before being rushed out of the hangar and back to my barracks room. Kelly had also been the family's sole point of contact for the police; they came to her home in Colorado to deliver the news of Kyle's suicide. Her mad dash to the airport was not unlike mine. Luckily, she had arrived two days prior, on Sunday evening, to meet Mom at Margie and Tim's.

"I wrote the eulogy," I whispered to Kelly, careful not to catch Mom's attention. She was busy making her coffee, but the woman can hear coffee grounds hit the floor. I slowly pulled the rumpled sheet of paper out of the front pocket of my jeans. I wanted Kelly to read it over to make sure it was coherent, and also that it faithfully captured the essence of Kyle Zalinsky.

"Oh, Kevin." Kelly covered her mouth with her free hand as she gripped the tear-blotted paper and strained to decipher my jumbled handwriting. "This is…It's perfect. Oh, look!" She pointed at the arrows connecting scattered song verses. "You even have lyrics from all the Beatles!"

"I wanted to get this right, Kelly. Kyle, he—"

"You *did* get it right," my sister assured me. She laid the paper flat on the top of her thigh and ironed out its wrinkles with her palm. "Thank you so much. I never could have written this. It's beautiful."

"What about everything else? The arrangements, the service, the burial?"

"Aunt Margie helped me make all those phone calls. She and Uncle Tim have been great, but..." Kelly leaned against the back of the couch and craned her neck to peer into the kitchen. "Just a head's up: Mom is going to want to go over to Kyle's apartment. And *you* need to take her."

"Leave it to the Favorite." I nudged her with an elbow and we shared a knowing little chuckle.

"Here, you guys. I noticed you haven't eaten any banana bread, so I made you a few sandwiches." Uncle Tim returned from the kitchen with a paper plate stacked with at least twenty-three sandwiches – just "a few." There was turkey, roast beef, pork roll, brisket, venison, honey ham, chicken salad, and I'm sure the rest of the barnyard gang buried in there somewhere. "I figured you guys needed something a little more substantial."

"Thanks, Uncle Meat!" I chirped, careful not to make an audible gagging sound lest I offend our gracious host. Kyle had a brief stint as a vegetarian when he was seventeen, and he lovingly nicknamed Uncle Tim "Uncle Meat" for his tendency to contribute a buffet of several different dead animals to family gatherings.

"I'll leave these right here. You kids don't forget to eat, now."

After Mom had a few cups of Folgers and a thirteenth piece of banana bread, we locked arms and headed out to her rental car in Margie and Tim's driveway. In a rare reversal of the status quo, Mom requested that *I* drive; she tossed me the keys and I opened the passenger door for her. Mom has always gotten a big kick out of watching me squeeze into the driver's seat anytime she had been the last to drive and the seat remains adjusted to accommodate her diminutive frame. In this scenario, I'm pressed fully against the steering wheel with very little in the way of wiggle room, so reaching down to move the seat backwards is a colossal pain in the ass. Every time, I'm reminded of Chris Farley's automotive struggles in *Tommy Boy:* "Fat guy in a little car!" What happened next has come to be known, in the annals of our family's illustrious history, as "the Fountain Incident."

"Come on, you son of a bitch!" I managed to just barely get my fingertips on the little lever that slides the seat back, and exhaled with great relief once my belly was free to expand. "Whew!"

"Honey, do you want to ask Pete to drive?" Mom asked, feigning concern through hearty laughter.

"No, Mom, I got this. I'm just gonna rest here for a second." I slumped against the back of the driver's seat and pretended to take a micronap with my eyes wide open. "I feel like a fucking zombie."

Mom snorted, startling herself. She raised a tissue-stuffed hand up to her mouth. "Don't make me laugh too hard, Kevin."

I should have heeded her warning. Instead, I lifted my arms straight out in front of me, lumbering corpse-style, and plopped my hands down on the top of the steering wheel. "Zombie," I groaned. "Driving zombie."

"Kevin, stop!" Mom was now literally choking back laughter. "All I've eaten for the past three days is that banana bread! My breath tastes like banana br—" Mom slammed her mouth shut, but not before a big burp squeezed itself out and made the entire car smell like funky bananas.

Then came the gurgle. I whipped my head in the general direction of her digestive system, unsure of the exact source of that disturbing sound. "Mom, where did that noise come from?"

"Oh, no…B-ban-banan-bananas!" Mom was wheezing so hard I could barely understand her. Her stomach started sloshing; she pressed her hands against the dashboard and braced herself.

"Mom?!" In my panic, I jumped out of the driver's seat, ran around the front of the car, and pulled open her door. Mom, laughing hysterically, nearly tumbled out of the car. "Should I call 911?"

For some reason, the idea of her son calling her an ambulance sent Mom off the deep end. I was convinced the banana bread had seeped into her brain, intoxicating her and making her delirious. She flung her feet out of the car and onto the pavement of the driveway. "Oh, God…It's happening."

Mom started spewing like a fountain.

Vomit splashed all over her blouse, all over her lap, all over her shoes, all over the driveway, and all over the inside of the passenger-side door. "Oh, my God!"

My screaming prompted Kelly, Margie, Tim, and Pete to come racing out of the house. "What's going on? Mom?!" Kelly ran at a full sprint across the front lawn, stopping dead in her tracks when she laid eyes on Mom the Human Vomit Fountain. "Jesus Christ!"

Mom was, unbelievably, *still laughing* as this chaos spilled forth from her throat.

"Go get your Aunt Kathy a towel!" Aunt Margie yelled at Pete, who tripped up the front steps in his hurry. Uncle Tim, bless his heart, was frozen in shock.

"Okay. Okay. I'm okay," Mom took a deep breath once the last of the liquified banana bread had exorcised itself from her body. "Phew!"

"Jesus, Mom!" I looked first at Mom's face, then at the putrid puddle pooling around her feet and the front passenger-side tire, and then at an equally mortified Kelly. "What the hell was *that?*"

"Here, Aunt Kathy!" Pete returned from the house with a ratty old washcloth and threw it on her lap from a safe distance.

"I'm gonna need more than *this!*" Mom laughed, waving the washcloth with a flick of the wrist. The rest of us jumped back so as to avoid any unintentional splatter.

As Aunt Margie led Mom back inside to get cleaned up, Kelly and I looked at each other with great concern, certain that the rest of the week would only continue in the downward spiral as encapsulated by the Fountain Incident. Uncle Tim, meanwhile, had unspooled the garden hose and was hosing down the driveway with a piddly trickle.

Chapter 17:
Family is Family

My breath was shallow; it came quicker and quicker until I was practically gasping for air. I willed myself to stave off the hyperventilation, but I knew it was only a matter of time. I was starting to panic. *"Am I getting enough oxygen? Am I breathing out enough carbon dioxide? Oh, my God. Is my breathing broken?"* My fingers were tingling. My palms were itchy. The tingling moved up to my forearms. *"Holy shit. Isn't this the sign of an oncoming stroke?"* I was getting hot. My palms had progressed from itchy to sweaty. The lower half of my face had gone numb. I was in the throes of full-blown hysteria. *"This is it. This is how I die."*

"Christ on a carousel!" Mom ran up to the car and ripped the passenger door open. "Let's *go*, Kevin! Your whole family is waiting for you!"

"Mom, I think I'm having a panic attack."

"Oh, you look fine to me. Come inside and have a glass of wine."

"Mom, I'm *really* nervous."

"Come on, Honey. I know you haven't been home in a long time, but just imagine how happy your family will be to see you on Thanksgiving! I mean, since you've been *deployed to the Middle East—*"

"Okay, let's go!" I staved off the inbound onslaught of Irish Catholic Guilt – I wouldn't have survived; Kelly may be good with guilt, but Mom trained at the side of the esteemed and revered Claire McCormick, so her guilt can *kill* – and followed Mom into Aunt Patty and Uncle Jake's farmhouse in Easton, Pennsylvania, where the entire McCormick clan was waiting to pounce and smother me with hugs, kisses, and their unconditional and unabated love. I was terrified.

"Oh, my Lord, it's Kevin!" An aunt, I think, cried out. I couldn't determine the source.

"Kevin! How are you?" at least fifteen McCormicks asked all at once.

"Let me get a look at my nephew!" Uncle Mike turned me in one direction as Uncle Dale pulled me in the opposite direction.

"Kevin! Come give your favorite cousin a hug!" I have thirteen cousins; I didn't know who I was expected to hug first.

I was overwhelmed by all this love and attention, and the mouthwatering aroma of the Thanksgiving cornucopia did little to calm me down. I hadn't smelled that in years, so the drool sputtered out of my mouth like a broken sprinkler.

"Okay! Okay! Let's give him a little space, people!" The seas of fair-skinned McCormicks parted and my *actual* favorite cousin, Kelsi, emerged like Moses in the desert to lead me to safety. "Hi, Kev." She gave me a tight squeeze with one arm and swatted away overeager relatives with the other.

"So, how have you been?" Kelsi asked once she'd rescued me from my loved ones and delivered me to the safety of the cousins' table in the corner of her parents' gigantic dining room. I was relieved to discover that the tradition of the cousins sitting separately from "the grown-ups" hadn't died in the ten years since I was last home for Thanksgiving. "It's been so long!"

"Yeah, ten years! I can't believe it! It's so nice to see everybody together and at least pretending to like each other."

That "contemporary cousins" fiasco from fifteen years prior started a chain reaction that would span an entire decade and hang in the atmosphere over four separate nuptials: *this person* wasn't invited to Bryce's ceremony so *that couple* was snubbed when it came time for Maureen to walk down the aisle, and so on and so forth. None of us cousins had anything to do with this pettiness; our parents were reigniting old feuds that should have disappeared like a puff of smoke back in the early Seventies. When it was Cliff's turn at the altar, he put his foot down and made it clear to his parents that *every* relative, even our recluse uncle who researches conspiracy theories on AOL in the Pocono mountains, would receive an invitation to his wedding. Thus was that domino effect of stupidity terminated.

"Yeah, they've finally stopped acting like big babies! For the most part, anyway. They're way too old to be that immature!" Kelsi pressed herself up against the table and whispered to me, "My mom has been driving me absolutely crazy since I've been home!"

"Aw, Aunt Patty? I love your mom! She's so sweet. *My mom* is the crazy one!"

"Aw, Aunt Kathy? I love your mom! She's so fun."

We heard Mom pop the cork on a fourth bottle of wine in the kitchen, prompting my teetotaling Baptist deacon Aunt Patty to start singing the praises of a nice glass of ice water, and wild cheers from everyone else. Kelsi and I exchanged a glance and burst into laughter.

"It *is* nice to hear them all having a good time together," Kelsi admitted. "But I want to hear about you! You've been in the Middle East for two years!"

"Yeah...I sure have." I had been back in America for less than forty-eight hours, and I still hadn't quite adjusted to, well, anything. The suburbs of New Jersey and Pennsylvania are a far cry from the deserts of Iraq and Syria. "It's great to be home. But I—"

"Kevin, just how hot is it *over there*?" My cousin Luke came bounding up behind me and shook my shoulders; I just about piddled myself.

"Uh...it's pretty hot. But it's a dry heat, so it's not that ba—"

"Is it true that the women *over there* have to be completely covered up or else they'll get *caned*?" My cousin Maureen was probably already on her sixth glass of chardonnay. "That's barbaric!"

"Well...that doesn't really happen in—"

"*God*, Maureen!" her sister Helena shouted from across the dining room. "It's called a burqa, and nobody gets *caned!* Unless they're in…Saudi Arabia or Afghanistan; I Googled it. Right, Kev?"

"Well, just as long as my nephew hasn't converted to that *Islam*." Uncle Joey pronounced it like "is-lamb" and I wanted to crawl under the table and die.

"Oh, Joe! Don't say ignorant things!" Aunt Carol smacked her husband on the back of his head. "…You *haven't* converted, right, Sweetie?"

"Careful now, Joe! Kevin knows their language; he might be an *insider!*" my Uncle Rick howled, before doing that thing that older men do where they jab the air in front of your face and then joggle your shoulders in an annoying expression of their love.

"That's *right!*" Aunt Carol exclaimed. "Wasn't it hard to learn that Arab language, Sweetie?" After five years of working on avionics in Hawaii, the Navy offered me a chance to study Arabic and become a translator. As a former kid from the vanilla suburbs of New Jersey, even *I* could comprehend the rarity of such an opportunity, so I accepted. Learning the language was tough; answering my relatives' silly questions as the family's subject matter expert was even tougher.

"Alright, everyone, quit bothering my nephew with all these stupid questions!" Aunt Francine pushed Joe, Carol, and Rick aside with a casserole dish before thrusting it into my face. "I made your favorite, Honey: maple sausage stuffing!"

"Well that can't *be*, Francine," Aunt Margie came rushing up behind Aunt Francine and pushed her casserole dish aside with her very own. "Because *I* made Kevin's favorite: green bean casserole!"

"Save that stuff for someone else, you two!" Aunt Debbie dashed across the dining room with – you guessed it! – a casserole dish containing my "actual" favorite. "Ambrosia! Made with extra fruit cocktail syrup, just how you liked it when you were little!"

"Uh…Kevin! Didn't you say you wanted a tour of the house? It *has* been ten years, right?" Thank God for my cousin Kelsi. She grabbed me by the wrist and pushed past the blockade of casserole dishes. We darted upstairs and hid from our aunts and their side dishes in her childhood bedroom. We sat cross-legged on the floor.

"Thanks! I love them, but…"

"It's overwhelming, huh?"

"A little." In the field, whenever I'd hear people talking rapidly or screaming excitedly, it wasn't ever directed at me; I'd be listening from a safe distance. Kelsi must have sensed my lingering anxiety.

"Hey, I'd be nervous, too, if a bunch of McCormicks surrounded me and started yelling in my face!" She laughed, nudging my crossed arms to loosen me up a little.

"And those *side dishes!* I can't tell Aunt Debbie that I hate her ambrosia; I'm gonna have to eat some."

"I *know!* Who lied to her and said all that fruit cocktail juice makes it good?! We'll just spit it out into our napkins."

"It'll be our little secret." I extended a pinky and Kelsi linked mine with hers.

"Pinky promise! No, wait…we need a stronger promise for this one!"

Kelsi and I looked each other in the eye and exclaimed, in unison, "Cousin promise!"

Uncle Mike delivered the keynote prayer when it came time for us to sit down for Thanksgiving dinner. It was another tradition I was happy to see alive and well. We stood in a tight circle in the kitchen around the spread of side dishes and the gargantuan turkey whose death would not be in vain, not on this day. "Before we load up our plates and feast on this bounty, may we join hands in a prayer of thanks."

Mom squeezed my hand in hers as Kelsi pushed a few McCormicks out of her way to hold my other one. "I love them all, but I'm holding your hand, dammit!" Kelsi whispered to me once she'd secured her spot, pressing against my shoulder and laughing.

"I'm so glad you're here, Honey." Mom leaned against my other shoulder. "Just think: in less than a year you'll be a civilian again and back home for good!"

"Let us bow our heads," Uncle Mike kicked off the invocation. "Lord, we ask you to bless this delicious food which we are about to enjoy. We thank you, oh Lord, for our beautiful family and the good fortune which allows us all to gather together today. We thank you for Patty and Jake, and their generosity in hosting all of us in their home, which has been the lovely setting for many a Thanksgiving celebration. We thank you for the joy which fills both the halls of this house and our hearts."

If it were socially acceptable among the diocesan crowd for priests to play golf every weekend, I have a feeling Uncle Mike would've chosen that for his profession instead of insurance salesman; the man delivers a prayer as masterfully as Arnold Palmer mixed iced tea and lemonade. "Lord, we thank you also for Kevin, who has safely returned to us – however briefly – from a very dangerous environment in order to join us, lift our spirits, and fill our hearts. We hope that he understands just how much he means to us."

In that moment, with Mom and Kelsi squeezing my hands and every last McCormick looking at me lovingly from around the prayer circle, my anxiety scattered like a wisp of sand on the desert wind.

Chapter 18:
Goodbye

"White trash coming through!" My Great Aunt Josephine – Auntie Josie for short, AJ for shorter – came bursting into the den with a big bowl of Chex Mix drizzled with honey and coated with powdered sugar – her signature "white trash."

MeeMaw and AJ had come up together from Hampton the week prior to see Dad. Well, actually, AJ caught wind that MeeMaw was coming up to see Dad, so she forced herself into MeeMaw's fuchsia Oldsmobile; that must have been *some* road trip. AJ is Pop-Pop's baby sister – MeeMaw's sister-in-law – and the two of them couldn't possibly be any different. MeeMaw was married just the once, for fifty-seven years to her true love; AJ was married four times, the last being, in her words, "strictly for the money, Honey." MeeMaw dressed about as conservatively as you'd expect an eighty-six-year-old woman to dress; AJ wore low-cut blouses, hip-huggers, stilettos, and only the most on-trend accessories. MeeMaw was sweet; AJ was sassy. MeeMaw loved Elvis; AJ thought the Ramones were "just the shit." I adored both of these women, but I'm not sure either would ever use the words "I adore" when referring to the other.

"Josephine, for goodness' sake, Johnny can't eat that stuff!" MeeMaw called from the kitchen.

"Oh, a little bit can't hurt!" AJ yelled back. "I know my most adorable great-nephew can't wait to have some of AJ's famous white trash! And Johnny, you have just a little nibble, okay? I want you to be happy and content!"

"Thanks, Josephine," Dad said meekly, lifting himself onto his elbows as AJ came over to place the bowl of white trash on his bedside table. She straightened his hair with one hand and placed the other on his cheek.

"My most handsome nephew-in-law! You've always been my favorite, Johnny." AJ lifted her arms to the sides and swept out of the room like a graceful ballerina dancing the part of a dramatic bird. She was a loving, affectionate woman who just so happened to have an extreme aversion to feeling sad, which she expressed in exaggerated ways.

"Kevin, keep your Auntie Josie away from me," Dad whispered once AJ was out of earshot. "She means well, but she's like Nurse Ratched."

"Sure thing, Dad." I adjusted his pillows after he dropped back down from his elbows. "Who's Nurse Ratched?"

"She's a scary nurse in *One Flew Over the Cuckoo's Nest*, and your dad is absolutely right, Honey. Let's keep her out of this room, okay?" MeeMaw closed the door behind her, shutting out the sound of AJ trilling some showtune in the kitchen. "Now, how's my favorite son-in-law doing?"

"Never better, Claire. Kevin is home with me," Dad retook my hand, which AJ's grand entrance had caused him to drop in surprise, and held MeeMaw's in his other. "Do you know your grandson made the dean's list?"

"Oh, Sweetie, that's great!" MeeMaw grabbed *my* other hand and squeezed it with her crooked little fingers. "Johnny, did you know that Kevin always gets the answers right whenever we watch *Jeopardy!* and *Wheel of Fortune* together? He's always been so smart!"

"Thanks, MeeMaw." My cheeks became flushed and hot; I felt so uncomfortable being the center of attention at a time like that.

"Now, let's get this *junk* out of here," MeeMaw snapped in a most unMeeMaw-like tone as she snatched up the bowl of white trash. "You don't need *this* sitting next to you."

"It's called 'white trash,' not 'junk,' Claire!" AJ called out from the kitchen before launching into her next performance.

"That woman can't hear the priest from the front pew, but she heard *that?*" MeeMaw whispered, prompting an unprepared Dad to burst into laughter. His hearty chuckle devolved into a hoarse cough. It must have been so hard on him to laugh, but I'll confess that it made me so happy to hear. It had been months. "Okay, Johnny, I'll let you rest. Take care of him, Sweetie."

Dad's face had become dried-out from dehydration during the white trash commotion. I went into his bathroom, ran a washcloth under some warm water, and wrung it out in the sink before returning to dampen his face. I looked at Dad once the fine layer of ash had been wiped away. His face was pallid and gaunt. The wrinkles that had once faintly framed his nose and mouth now carved deep lines through his cheeks. I wished it were possible to wipe away those hard lines with the washcloth, just as easily as dirt. The few freckles that had dotted Dad's cheeks in healthier days had faded entirely into the pale. His skin was almost transparent, like that of a papier-mâché mask in the early stages of assembly. And yet Dad was handsome, even in this grim state. He struggled to keep his eyes open; his eyelids, heavy and dark with exhaustion, fluttered as he looked at me. But his were the same beautiful blue eyes I had always known. Those kind, gentle, serene eyes: I hoped they were reflecting even a fragment of what Dad saw when he looked at me.

"Are you okay, Dad?

"Yes, Son."

"You're comfortable? Do you have enough pillows? Is this blanket warm enough?"

"Yes, yes, and yes, Son."

"Do you want me to adjust the thermostat at all?"

"No, Son."

"Are you sure you don't want—" I pointed at his feeding machine, its unplugged cord wrapped around the stand and draped over the monitor. An unopened can – next in the nutrition lineup – collected dust on the floor next to the machine.

"I'm sure, Son."

I'm certain some hidden, subconscious part of me was relieved; every time I'd crack open one of those sour-smelling cans, Dad would retch, so I would retch, and I'd be tempted to throw the can through the window and into the neighbor's backyard. Sometimes Dad would even egg me on. Of course, we couldn't do that, so I'd hold my breath and pour the can's contents into the pouch of the feeding pump. Dad would usually fall asleep to the rhythmic clicking and whirring, waking only if he turned his head and caught a whiff of the vapors.

A few hours earlier, Dad said "No more." No more feeding machine. No more cans of nutrients. No more pills. No more injections. No more.

"It's my time," he'd said in such a matter-of-fact, resigned way that Kyle burst into tears and fled the room. I had never once seen my brother so overcome with emotion. Kelly followed close behind to make sure he was okay, and Mom, well – Mom was Mom. She busied herself with cleaning: first she vacuumed the living room, next she dusted the dining room, and then she scrubbed down the bathroom before moving on to organizing the pantry. Every so often, Dad and I would hear the dull *clang* of an aluminum can in the kitchen.

"Your mom, she…I guess she's taking this as well as she can."

"She's taking it better than Kyle."

"Your brother is sensitive right now. He hasn't been here with me for three months like you have. This is hard on him."

"Time hasn't made this any easier to deal with," I'd wanted to say, but Dad didn't need an ounce of my truculent teenage attitude, especially not now. I had been back since December. Up until then, Mom had been paying a visiting nurse to come five times a week and check on Dad while she worked. Cancer is much too expensive for a single-income family; Mom had reached both her wit's and savings account's end between paying the nurse, paying the bills,

paying the mortgage, and keeping her husband alive. But "alive" is impossible to maintain on five two-hour visits a week. When I came home for Christmas break and saw for myself the severity of the situation, I didn't have a choice, Favorite or not: I dropped out of school and moved back home to take care of Dad. The dean's list doesn't mean shit when your father is dying from cancer.

I realized, during the course of those three months as I watched him waste away in front of me, that I hadn't appreciated Dad in the innumerable ways he had deserved. Here was a decent, hard-working, patient, humble, quiet, considerate man who had never boasted or acted out of pettiness or called us names or drank too much or ran around on Mom or beat us or walked out on us or, hell, flipped someone the bird when they cut him off without using their goddamn blinker. And yet, he was dying from cancer at the age of sixty. I tried to come to terms with it, as Dad himself had when he said "No more; it's my time," but those were terms I just couldn't accept. And, as he became bonier and frailer, my frustration grew into a humongous, unruly, terrifying thing. The cans of foul sludge didn't make him stronger; the medicine didn't relieve his pain; fresh sheets and a clean diaper didn't make him comfortable. Cancer was winning this war, despite my best efforts. My fight just wasn't good enough.

"Don't beat yourself up, Son," Dad said, snapping me out of my self-reproach. He knew me all too well.

"I'll try not to, Dad." The levee holding back the flood had started to crumble; tears were snaking their way through the cracks. "I'm sorry."

"You have nothing to be sorry for, Kevin." Dad's voice was growing thin. "You've done so much for me."

"*But was it enough?*"

"And it was *more* than enough. You put college on hold for your old man. Now, I need you to promise me—"

I shook my head furiously. I didn't like where this conversation was headed; we must have taken a wrong turn somewhere. "Dad, don't," is all I could manage.

"Promise me that you'll finish your education. Don't be a dumb Marine like your dad and not go to school. Promise?"

"I promise," I mouthed. I couldn't speak at this point. I squeezed Dad's hand with both of mine as confirmation. His hand felt like a dense lump of clay in my hands, but featherlight, too, like it might float away if I didn't hold tight.

"Good. Now, give me a kiss and send Mom in, okay?" I kissed Dad on the forehead. As I drew away from him he patted me on the head, just as if I were a kid again. "Oh, and Kevin?" He called out before I shut the door behind me. His eyes were closed. "Take care of your brother while I'm gone, okay? He'll need you."

I found Mom in the kitchen, leaning up against the island with her hands flat on the countertop. Classic Kathy: she was telling a story. Several McCormicks – I hadn't even been aware that anybody else had arrived, and I can't remember who was in attendance in the audience – had gathered around to hear Mom's tale.

"I met John on New Year's Eve, nineteen…seventy-nine. Well, I didn't *meet* him, but I spoke to him. Donna and Freddie were having their usual New Year's Eve party – it was always a really big deal – but I was working the night shift at Warren Hospital, so I couldn't go. Donna called, but I was on my rounds, so one of the other nurses left a note for me to call her back. So, I did, on my next break. She answered the phone when I called, and I could hear them having a wild time in the background – you know, good music, lots of dancing, laughing, drinking – and Donna goes 'Everybody say hi to Kathy!' and I heard people screaming 'Happy New Year, Kathy!' I'm sure most of them had no idea who I was.

"So, when all that noise died down, Donna said 'Kathy, there's a guy here who I think you'd really like' – Donna was always trying to set me up with one of Freddie's buddies so we could go on double dates – and she goes 'His name is John, but everybody calls him Goofy.' And right away I thought, 'Wait a minute, now…I don't know if I can be seen going out with a guy who people call Goofy,' but I gave him a chance because Donna vouched for him. So, we talked, and…he seemed like a nice guy. I could tell he had a sense of humor, which was always the number one thing for me. A lot of guys in Jersey in the Seventies didn't really have a sense of humor – it wasn't 'cool' – so it was nice that he wasn't like those other guys.

"Anyway, we were talking for quite a while – my break was long over by the time I finally hung up the phone – and I remember John saying, 'You know, I'm the very first person you talked to in the Eighties,' so I looked at the clock, and he was right: it was past midnight. I hadn't even realized it! I can't remember hearing the countdown, or the New Year's song, or people screaming and cheering; I must have blocked it all out. So then John goes 'That's good luck for me! If I ask you out on a date, you'll say yes.' So, he asked me out on a date and…I said yes. We made plans to go out sometime the following week; I think we went to Key City Diner.

"He made me laugh. From the very beginning, John has made me laugh. We sat in that diner booth for almost three hours – just *laughing* – before the waitress came over and kicked us out. They were closing, and it was starting to snow. I remember how pretty the snow was, falling past the streetlights outside the diner, as John walked me to my car. And I remember just feeling so…*happy* as I drove home that night. I can't remember feeling that way before I met John. And he has never, in twenty-six years, made me feel any different than I did on that night. And…that's why I love him."

The kitchen was silent. Hell, even AJ was speechless. If not for the sniffling here and there, I would have forgotten that anybody else was in that room. MeeMaw gently pulled Mom away from the island and towards her. She wiped the tears from Mom's cheeks with the tissue she had pinched between her crooked fingers.

"Mom?" She was still outside that diner in 1980. I felt like such an asshole for calling her back to the present. "Dad's looking for you."

"Okay, Honey." MeeMaw took her by the hands and silently encouraged her – such was the power of MeeMaw that her rallying cries required no words whatsoever – before sending Mom on her way to Dad. I had an image in my head then of Mom as a little freckle-faced spitfire, being comforted by her mother in the same wordless way. Mom gave me a kiss on the cheek as she passed. "Thank you, Honey."

MeeMaw hobbled over to me and took my hands in hers, followed first by AJ, who rested her head on my shoulder, and then by Aunt Debbie, who hugged me from the side and pressed her cheek against my other shoulder. They were telling me what I had known the second I pulled the den door shut behind me: it was time. I looked into the living and dining rooms and saw that they had become standing room only, filled to bursting with every last living McCormick, along with quite a few second cousins and family friends I hadn't seen before and I haven't seen since. I'm sure the dead McCormicks were all there, too: marveling at how much we'd all grown; hugging those they had left behind; and dancing in midair, careful not to spill Dad's pint of cold beer. Under any other circumstances, this would've been a joyous sight and a cause for celebration. But not today: they had gathered to say goodbye.

Mom was in with Dad for probably an hour. I stood in the kitchen doorway, catty-corner to the den, arms crossed and chin pressed into my chest. I heard Mom climb into the adjustable single bed with Dad; I pictured her laying her head on his frail chest. I heard whispers, muffled sobs, and Mom's sporadic laughter which tore sharply through their hushed exchange. I wondered what inside jokes they were retelling, what old secrets they were recalling, what new promises they were making to each other. As they looked back on their life together with a weathered perspective, I hoped that Mom and Dad remembered how they had felt on that snowy night in January 1980. I hoped that the fond memories far outweighed the bad.

More than once I could hear Mom ask, with a tremble in her hoarse voice, "Why?" and Dad would respond only with "I love you,

Kathy." He didn't have the answer to that pressing question, but he did know when the time had arrived. I heard the bed creak and the patter of Mom's feet on the hardwood floor as she crossed to the door. She opened it and nodded at the McCormicks, who lined up single-file, wrapping around the dining room table, along the wall between the fireplace and the living room sofa, past the staircase, and into the kitchen; the last McCormick was backed up against the door to the backyard.

The McCormicks and our *extended* extended family filed into the den and managed to squeeze fifty people into a room with a rated maximum capacity of twelve. They took turns leaning over the railing of that rented hospital bed and pressing themselves into Dad – straightening his hair and wiping their tears from his terrycloth robe after they'd pull away – telling him "I love you, Johnny boy," and "You were always my favorite, Uncle John." Dad would just smile and say "I love you; please don't cry."

Kyle sat on his left side, holding Dad's hand up against his flushed cheek; Kelly stretched one arm across Kyle's back and wedged the other between Dad's shoulders and the headboard; Mom sat to Dad's right and dabbed his face with the damp washcloth; and I sat at his feet, holding tight to his other hand with both of mine. Dad reminded Mom how, when he was gone, he didn't want to be shoved into a casket and buried underground; he wanted to be cremated. He joked, "Leave enough room for yourself, Kathy, but please don't stick your boyfriends' ashes in there with me." We all ugly laughed through the tears and snot.

"Don't worry, John," Mom assured him. "We'll get you a nice urn and put you on the mantle in the living room. That way, you won't miss anything; you'll be where the action is."

"I'm not worried, Dear; I know you'll fill me in on everything eventually."

"We'll keep Kathy out of trouble, John," Uncle Mike promised.

"Yeah, Johnny," added Uncle Dale. "Wish us luck! Even four brothers and a sister might not be enough to keep Kathy out of trouble!"

Everyone in the den nodded in agreement and laughed. I heard the crinkling of several dozen packs of Kleenex.

"We'll take good care of the kids, too, Johnny!" Aunt Carol chimed in, reaching out to grab me by the shoulder and Kyle by his.

Kyle and I shared a commiserating look. For the first time in my life, I saw Dad in Kyle's face. Growing up, everyone would remark in astonishment how much I looked like Mom and Kyle like Dad, but I could never see it. Until that moment; there were Dad's eyes, and his eyebrows, and the crease between his eyebrows, and his nose, and his chin, and the cleft in his chin. I wondered if Dad looked into Kyle's face and saw a reflection of himself as a younger man, or perhaps a reflection of the way he imagined himself up until even then, his final day. In those last moments, with his entire five-person family piled into that single bed and surrounded by – of all people – dozens of his in-laws, I saw the peace in Dad's eyes.

And I watched the peace leave, gradually and then all at once. But it didn't just *leave*: it left with Dad. His eyes – so full of light – became like dull glass in that moment, and my heart sank like I had never felt before. That feeling, that dreadful *thud* when my heart lost its bearings and collided against the wall of my chest, is one I pray to never again experience. It was a mortifying sensation, and I fear, even in this very moment, that to think about it is to risk drawing it back into existence like some terrible demon.

Dad died at eight forty-three p.m. on March 10th, 2006 – a month shy of my nineteenth birthday. Dad, putting others before himself until the bitter end, couldn't very well leave without first giving me a few gifts. As far as presents go, there were only nineteen years' worth: he taught me how to forgive, how to take my time, how to love the one you're with, how to stack the charcoal so your burgers cook evenly, how to keep a cool head and an even keel, how to put others' needs ahead of your own without hesitation, how to just do your best and be proud of yourself for it, how to give away your love with just a look, how to move through a crowd without ever pushing or shoving, how to find contentment in even the quietest moments, how to be a good man and a decent human being, and how to pack five peoples' luggage into a station wagon and still leave room in the way back for the Favorite.

Chapter 19:
Let It Be

"Well, Kyle, I guess you're really gone."

I sat at the foot of my brother's bed, flicking the program from his funeral service against the frame. As I was waiting to deliver Kyle's eulogy, I must have folded and unfolded that program at least three hundred times; it provided durable fodder for my nerves. An enormous poster of a close-up of John Lennon's face took up almost the entire wall across from his bed; he stared down at me, and I stared back at him. His eyes, unavoidable at this extreme closeness, reminded me so much of Kyle's: a mischievous glint on the surface, pulling focus from a discontent hiding in plain view just beyond. That was Kyle to a T. Same shit-eating grin, too.

Paul McCartney sat backwards in a wooden chair on a smaller poster under John. "Don't feel too bad, Paul." I could relate; growing up, I often felt overshadowed by my brother and his antics. I recalled the evening I had planned on coming out to my family: he flipped his shit *and* the couch all because Dad said "no." But there was no space for resentment or bitterness. There wasn't room for much else besides exhaustion. I hadn't slept at all on the flight from Japan, nor was I able to get much sleep at Aunt Margie and Uncle Tim's. I was so worried about Mom. I could hear her pacing the floor and blowing her nose in the middle of the night; she must have been crying herself to sleep every night.

I spotted a framed magazine cover featuring George Harrison on Kyle's bookshelf, but I couldn't find Ringo Starr anywhere. "Poor Ringo. Oh, wait – there you are." I noticed a postcard, peeking out from underneath a stack of issues of *Rolling Stone*, which featured the *Let It Be* album cover. "You made it in after all, Ringo." Also on the shelves were books of Beatles lyrics, Lennon biographies, a few books written by John himself – *In His Own Write* and *A Spaniard in the Works* were two of Kyle's favorite books, although I could never get very far with either before giving up and putting them back on the shelf – and a bobblehead of Tom Petty, but *The Simpsons'* version of Tom Petty. Looking around that room, one would be forgiven for assuming that it belonged to some former roadie who gave up the hard stuff to become a vinyl purist and collector of tchotchkes.

On the floor between the bookshelf and Kyle's closet was a stack of history books, most of them about the Revolutionary War and the Thirteen Colonies. "Do you remember when Dad took us down to Williamsburg that one summer? I guess we were…twelve and fifteen? That was fun. I don't think you punched me *once!* You were too busy acting like a tour guide and giving me history lessons about *everything*. But it was nice to see you in your element like that." Cartoon Tom Petty was staring at me with a big toothy grin, absolutely enthralled by my story. "That's right! That's the summer you introduced me to Tom Petty and the Heartbreakers. You played their greatest hits on the road trip down to Virginia. And on the way back it was…Roy Orbison, I think?" I didn't see a trace of Roy in Kyle's room; that must have been a very short phase.

As much as Kyle loved history, his one true passion was music, specifically rock 'n' roll. An acoustic guitar was propped against the other side of the bookcase. I imagined him sitting in the exact same spot where I sat, strumming his guitar and singing to himself. I wondered which song he last played on that guitar. Had he played it the night before, or maybe even an hour before he killed himself? "Why did you stop playing, Kyle? You should have just kept on playing." What was the last song he listened to? I hoped it was one of his favorites. "Did you listen to it in the car on your way to that goddamn bridge? Did you sing along to it? Why didn't it make you want to stop your car and turn around?"

An electric guitar with four snapped strings had been laid on top of a crate containing dozens of records next to Kyle's bed. He used to enjoy acting out his strung-out rock star fantasy and furiously shred on that thing, as if he had the money to be constantly repairing it. Once, during a high school talent show, Kyle and his band – I think they were called something ridiculous like the Rubber Nipples – performed *Revolution* by the Beatles and Kyle was so moved by the Holy Spirit that he smashed his guitar on the stage and spit on it. Mom and the principal of his school, in a rare instance of being on the same page about anything Kyle-related, were both pissed. If Kyle would be practicing in his room at some late hour on a school night, I'd scream "Shut the fuck up!" from across the hall, and he'd scream back "Rock and roll never sleeps, Goddammit!" Good times.

I reached over to pull the guitar off the box of records, and laid it behind me on the bed. I dragged the crate towards my feet and started rifling through it. James Brown, Joan Jett, Willie Nelson, the Rolling Stones— *Exile on Main Street*. I nearly dropped the record. My shoulders and heart sank in unison. "Your desert island album. Shit." I realized immediately my egregious oversight: I hadn't played it, start to finish, at Kyle's funeral. "Shit. Shit. How could I have forgotten? The *one* goddamn thing you asked me to do." My hope was that Kyle had long forgotten his request, that when he came down from his high, the thought dissipated like a purple haze. But that didn't offer me much comfort; after all, I was able to recall it the second I laid eyes on that album cover. "I let you down, Kyle. I'm sorry. But I'll bet you're listening to it right now, aren't you?"

I clutched *Exile* to my chest and flopped backwards onto the bed, careful not to bang my head against Kyle's guitar. I watched the orange light stretch across the ceiling of his bedroom as the sun set; I could hardly believe that the day was almost over. The seconds had seemed to be reveling in my family's misery, wringing out every last excruciating drop of the stuff before reluctantly moving on. And yet, the day of Kyle's funeral had mercifully rushed by. The exhaustion had started to make its presence painfully known, creeping up my body and squeezing itself in between my joints. Oddly enough, my elbows are always the first to be hit by fatigue; I could barely stand to keep my arms folded in a hug around Kyle's vinyl.

My eyelids had gotten heavy. My eyes were closed for only a few minutes before I heard the jangling of a bicycle bell on the street below Kyle's apartment. I was reminded of the time some kid stole my bike after I had fallen off of it. I was probably nine; I was leaving a pool party at my friend Martin's house. Mom had sent

Kyle down the block to tell me it was time to come home. I hopped on my bike, not realizing that the towel I had thrown around my neck had come undone and was dangling loosely down my back. I made it past a few houses before the towel got caught in the spokes of my bike's tire, yanking me backwards and flinging me face-first onto the sidewalk. As I sobbed and checked for missing teeth, some big kid stood my bike up, walked it over my battered legs, and proceeded to ride off on it. Well, he tried to, anyway.

"Hey! That's my brother's bike, you fucker!" Although Kyle hadn't immediately sprang off his bike when he saw me get thrown from mine, he sure as shit wasn't about to let this burly bully make off with it.

"Finders keepers, asshole!" The thief should have concerned himself more with getting a decent head start, and less with goading someone with a notoriously short fuse. As he wobbled down the sidewalk on his new too-small bicycle, Kyle raced after him on foot. When he caught up with him, Kyle grabbed the thief by the back of the neck like a mother cat might snatch up her young. He hurled the kid into the middle of the street, and the bike continued on its own for a few seconds before falling onto its side in a neighbor's front lawn.

"Fucker," Kyle mumbled as his vanquished foe crawled to safety between two parked cars. "Get your bike, Kevin."

"I…was amazed. I guess I was expecting you to make fun of me because I wasn't wearing a shirt and my fat was exposed. And wet. Instead…you were like my hero in that moment." I wondered what I had done so wrong to not deserve more moments like that. "No…No, I'm sorry. I need to stop playing the victim. There were others."

"Alright, Kyle. I guess now is as good a time as any to tell you this. It's my own damn fault. I could've been an adult and told you a lot sooner than…right now.

"Do you remember when, after Dad died, those people from the hospice came to pick up the bed, and the feeding machine, and the unused cans of food, and Dad's medicine? Well…they didn't take the bottle of pills that Dad kept in the bathroom. You know how much that idea scared him – that he'd drag himself all the way to the bathroom, only to realize that he forgot his medicine on the table next to his bed, so he'd have to drag himself all the way back to get it – so he kept a bottle of pills in the bathroom just in case.

"Anyway, I found those pills after the people left; the bottle was practically full. I didn't know what else to do with it, so…I took it upstairs to my room. I…I was in a really bad place. I felt like I had failed Dad. I felt like he died because…because I didn't try hard enough. I really beat myself up over it.

"A few days later, I was…I guess I was depressed. But not just depressed. I was…I was ready to kill myself. I was sitting on my bed, holding that bottle of pills in my hand and just staring at it. I didn't know what the hell they were, but I figured if I took enough of them, they'd kill me. My mind was made up. I was going to do it. My hand was on the cap of that bottle – I was *in the process* of twisting it off, Kyle.

"And then you barged into my room. Mom had me move the computer into my room because you were always downloading music and she was worried you'd get arrested, do you remember? So, you barged into my room and you said 'I need to use the computer.' I don't think you even looked at me; you just sat down at my desk and logged in to Instant Messenger. I think you were gonna message your girlfriend.

"So, I…I threw that bottle of pills behind me and I pulled my blanket over it real quick. And I sat there, on my bed – you were just hammering away at that keyboard, not paying me any attention – and I remember thinking to myself, 'You don't want to kill yourself. If you really wanted to kill yourself, you wouldn't have felt…you wouldn't feel so relieved right now.'

"I was *relieved* that you had barged into my room. You know how much I hated that. I was always screaming 'Knock first, God damn it!' But I was so glad to see you then. I was happy to toss those pills,

175

to get them out of my hands, out of my sight. I didn't want to kill myself. *You* made me realize that. *You* stopped me from doing something that I wouldn't be able to undo. You saved my life, Kyle."

Why couldn't he let me do the same thing for him?

"There's always been space between us. Of course, when I'm halfway across the world – in Hawaii, or Japan, or India – but even when we're together, in the same room. You could feel it, too, couldn't you? I think we kept each other at a distance because…why? Because we were afraid of getting hurt? Why were we so worried about hurting each other? I know things weren't always great when we were kids, but…I think we were making some real progress. I was feeling good about our relationship. I felt, for the first time, like…like I loved you.

"I still love you, Kyle. I don't understand why you did it. I'm mad at you for leaving us this way. I'm especially mad that you left Mom this way. I mean, we *just* lost Dad. But I have no room to talk. I mean…I thought about doing it myself. I wouldn't be here, right now…in *your* room, surrounded by *your* stuff…if it hadn't been for you. Maybe if you knew what you had done for me, you wouldn't have…well, I don't know. I just wish I had known what was going on. Maybe I could have helped you, too.

"Do you remember Christmas…when was it, three years ago? Mom and Kelly had gone to bed, and you and I stayed up and drank in the kitchen? Normally, I'd dread being left alone with you, because…I never knew what to say, or how we'd pass the time without feeling awkward. But…surprisingly, it wasn't awkward at all. Well, maybe a little bit, when we start making those promises to each other.

"I said, 'I promise not to call you stupid' and you said, 'I promise not to call you fat.' You know, dumb promises that like that didn't even really apply to us anymore. But then…you promised me that you'd be a better brother to me, and I promised the same thing to you. Do you remember that? I think we might have hurried through that part of the conversation, but I remember it. I think of that night pretty often.

"And then I did things like not respond to your texts for a few days, or even a few weeks. And not pick up the phone and call you. I don't know what we'd talk about, but we could at least have said 'Hi, how are you, hope things are well.' The last time we talked was on Christmas, for crying out loud. And it's...it's fucking *May*. That's bullshit, Kyle. We had time for everybody else in our lives, but...our only brother? No, we didn't have five minutes to spare for him. I promised you that I'd be a better brother, but I'm not sure I held up my end of the bargain.

"I love you. I love you so much more than I thought I did. I feel so...so *gutted* right now. I never realized I could possibly miss you this much. But I do. I miss you, and you...you're gone. You're the only person I've ever come out to, you know. Not Kelly, not Mom, not Dad...I'm sure he knows now, and I'm sure he doesn't give a shit, but I never told him. I had planned on doing it the summer after you graduated from high school, but things started getting...pretty bad for him. I need you to take care of Dad up there, Kyle. Give him a big hug for me, okay? You and Kelly always called me 'the Favorite,' but, if you ask me, I think *you* might've been Dad's favorite. I mean, you drove him absolutely fucking crazy – remember the Couch Incident, and the Chinese delivery guy, and the Ford Focus? – but you had a lot in common; I think Dad saw a lot of himself in you. So you take care of him! Take care of MeeMaw and Pop-Pop, too, while you're at it. It's a lot to ask, but...well, you're there.

"One more thing – I promise – before I let you go. Something happened to me about a year ago. Something I don't like to think about, something I...I don't think I can say out loud. But I think you can see it now. Isn't that how this works? You pass over to the other side, and you suddenly know everything, right? Um...Well...Sorry I didn't think to give you a head's up. I just want you to know that...um...after it happened...I said to myself, 'Kevin, if you didn't kill yourself after Dad died...you won't kill yourself after this.' And that's…that's thanks to you, Kyle. You saved my life – *twice* – and you didn't even know it. Well…now you know it.

"I'm gonna need your help. Your brother's a little messed up – surprise! I need…Whatever you can do with your new angel powers to help me out, that would be great. Can you do that for me? Well, I guess you need time to get situated, to get adjusted to your new…life. So…take your time. I love you, Kyle."

I sat up and wiped the tears from my face. The sun had just about fully set, and shadows now stretched along the ceiling. I put *Exile on Main Street* back where I had found it, and returned the box of records and electric guitar to where they belonged. I said goodbye to John, then Paul, then George, then Ringo, then Tom, and then – even though he wasn't there – to Roy. I stood up and looked out his bedroom window, and saw Kelly waiting in the rental car in the parking lot of Kyle's apartment complex. She had dropped me off for a few minutes before going to check on Mom, who rode back with Aunt Margie and Uncle Tim after the funeral. We had thoroughly cleaned the car since the Fountain Incident, so I wasn't too worried about Kelly choking on the smell of days-old vomit. She was chatting away on her phone, probably to my brother-in-law, so I had a few minutes yet.

In his room, surrounded by his albums, and his books, and his collectibles, and his guitars, and his *stuff*, I felt Kyle hugging me goodbye. "I love you, Kevin," I was certain he was saying to me, freed from whatever trivial constraints which made it so hard for him to say it when we existed in the same sphere. I, too, had been set free; I wasn't ashamed to say "I love you, too" into the void, nor was I disheartened when I didn't hear a response, because I just *knew*. Kyle and I had advanced to a new place of understanding, our souls intertwined in a way that would have been otherwise impossible. That amounts to only a tiny bit of consolation, however, and it certainly doesn't mean that I don't miss him being *here*. For now, though, he belongs to a different place: on some far astral plane, I can imagine him strumming his guitar, and singing his favorite Beatles songs, and unscrewing a never-ending string of Christmas lights, and pranking his fellow incorporeal beings while wearing that signature smirk of his, and at peace.

Chapter 20:
The Big Bang

"My mom has this plan – she calls it her 'Big Bang theory' – for when she gets old and feels the incompetence and senility coming on. She says she's going to stand on the side of a busy street, and when she sees a bus coming along, she'll step off the curb just in time and – *bang!* Mom refuses to become a burden on her kids. Well…on me, really, since my sister would never take her in."

"Now *that's* certainly an…interesting plan. How do you feel when your mother talks about that sort of thing?"

"Well, my mom has always had a twisted sense of humor – I think that's where I get it from – so I'm not too worried when she makes jokes like that. She also tells me to put lipstick on her and change her underwear before I call 911, if I'm the one who discovers her dead body. She doesn't want to be seen by strangers wearing dirty underwear or no lipstick. That's just the kind of stuff we joke about."

"I *have* noticed that you're able to joke around and make light of some pretty heavy stuff. That's not necessarily a bad thing; humor is often used effectively as a coping mechanism. We just want to be careful not to treat certain traumas as a joke."

"I know…But sometimes I make jokes at inappropriate times, without meaning to or even realizing it…and I feel like people might think that I'm morbid, or not taking whatever it is seriously."

"And this is an inherited trait, I'm starting to gather. Again, it's not a bad thing: we all need to deal with our pain in a way that's appropriate for *us*, as individuals. But you say you're not bothered when your mom tells you about her – what was it? – 'Big Bang theory?'"

"No, not really. Mom laughs every time she talks about it, so I know – or I *hope*, at least – that it's just a joke. What *does* bother me, though…"

"Talk to me about it."

"Thinking about my mom getting old…getting sick…*dying*. That just…It brings me right back to my dad. I watched my dad get sick and die, and…I don't think I'd be able to handle seeing the same thing happen to Mom."

"That's a completely understandable concern to have. It's always a difficult thing to consider our parents' mortality; as they get older, they move further and further away from the image of them that we've held for our entire lives."

"Yeah, and I don't want the last image I have of Mom to be her collapsed on the kitchen floor in dirty underwear…which I'd then have to change."

"You were young when your father died, and it wasn't fair – not for your father, not for your family, not for you. Those circumstances were quite difficult. But you were there for him; you did so much to for him. And I do sincerely hope that you recognize that."

"I do…I know that I did my best for Dad. It's just…it really sucks that my best wasn't good enough."

"You know, our 'best' just isn't always a match for cancer. Cancer is resilient, it's relentless, it's brutal…it's very hard to overcome. But I guarantee you that, whatever you did for your dad, it was the absolute most that you could have done. And you told me how he was so appreciative, how he thanked you for all that you had done for him. Isn't that right?"

"Yeah. Dad…Dad was so thankful. He acted like it was such a huge deal that I stayed home to take care of him, but…I did it without a second thought. And I hope that he never felt like he was any kind of burden on me."

"I'm sure he didn't feel that way; he knew exactly how much he meant to you. You were his best friend, after all, weren't you?"

"Yeah…I was. I adored that man. He was always there for me, he always cheered me on, he was always so interested in whatever it was that I had going on…I mean, I had a no-name ensemble part in *West Side Story* when I was a freshman in high school, and Dad, he…he acted like I had a starring role. He'd yell my name every single time he spotted me in the background – and sometimes he could only see my shoes behind the curtain – and he was *so proud* of me. He just…he always loved me. And he was *funny*, too, up until the very end; I told you about his 'Dr. Finklefinger' jokes. I was so lucky to have him in my life."

"From the sounds of it, your dad was pretty lucky, too: he had you."

"Thanks. That's…nice to hear. I'm just…I'm glad that I'm able to talk about Dad without breaking down into a blubbering mess. It's taken me years to get here."

"And you should be proud of yourself for it. Even if it's taken some time, at least you've arrived at this point."

"I am. I am proud of myself. I beat myself up for *years* over my dad dying, but…I realize that it wasn't my fault. Dad was the best person I've ever known, and…I understand now that bad things just sometimes happen to good people. It is what it is. I have to always remind myself of the good times."

"That's a great strategy to employ: think of the good times you and your dad shared; think more of all those happy memories and less of the sad ones. You don't deserve to be bogged down by negativity, or regret, or sadness. Those burdens do nothing but keep you fastened to the past and unable to enjoy the here and now."

"And it's not fair to my mom and sister. We all need to stick together – now more than ever – so I need to make sure that I'm here for them, one hundred percent."

"That's a wonderful way to remind yourself of your worth, of your importance, of the love you inspire and deserve. But always remember, Kevin: you have your mom and your sister, just like they have you. Don't be afraid to use your support system, to lean on your family. You've had to be so strong for your loved ones on several occasions, but there's absolutely *no* weakness in relying on and drawing strength from them, too."

"I know. I just *really* don't want to let them down. I…I feel like I let Kyle down, and I don't wanna do that again."

"It's tough, Kevin. Suicide is always such a difficult thing to come to terms with. But, if you remind yourself that—"

"I don't…I'm not sure if I'm ready to talk about that. Not yet."

"I understand, Kevin. Why don't we stop here, then? We've covered a lot today."

"Okay. Thanks."

"The next time we meet, we can talk more about your brother, and also about what happened in Hawaii. I *do* think we ought to spend more time addressing that one."

"Why did you even have to bring that up? This poor lady already has enough of my sad shit to sift through. And Kyle…that alone is gonna take four or five sessions to deal with. Hopefully she forgets about it before next time."

"Don't worry; I've taken plenty of notes for next time. And I'd like you to take the time until we next meet to really think about these things and how they're affecting you."

"Okay, I will."

"And, please, Kevin – don't wait too long before you come back and talk to me. I'm sure we can fit you in sometime within the next few weeks. Don't stay away for four months, okay?"

* * *

I got home to my new apartment in downtown Denver just in time for the movers. They had given me a four-hour delivery window and arrived *before* the window. When the hell does that ever happen? I was fully expecting them to show up within the last fifteen minutes.

"Petty Officer Zalinsky?"

"Not since about two months ago, but hi, how are you?"

"I'm good, thanks. We've got your stuff from Bahrain here. You ready?"

I nodded yes, and thus began the parade of *stuff*: the Turkish lamps and handwoven rugs I'd picked up from the souks of Manama; the pottery, trinkets, and knife – personalized with my Arabic name, "Karim" – that I'd smuggled out of Qatar; my kuma and massar, those fly traditional Omani headdresses; the beer steins I picked up during my brief stay in Germany, one of which features a busty fräulein in a skimpy dirndl playing peek-a-boo with a shirtless Aryan hunk while a drunk bear climbs a windmill in the background; and boxes and boxes of the tacky sweat-wicking workout gear I'd worn as regular clothes in Bahrain out of sheer desperation.

"Where do you want these two?"

"Oh, right in here is fine." I gestured towards the empty bedroom and the mover followed behind me with two small cardboard boxes stacked in his tattooed arms. One of the boxes was just the contents of my junk drawer in Manama, but the other one contained the dozens of pictures Mom had given me when I was home for Thanksgiving. It was a veritable treasure trove for me, but just more *stuff* to unload as far as the mover was concerned. I couldn't blame him; nobody really cares about a stranger's Eighties memories preserved in a pile of Polaroids. "Thanks."

I didn't have a pair of scissors – I never seem to have the appropriate tool handy for any given task, and I even told myself "Make sure you buy a pair of scissors, or steal some from Kelly, before the movers get there" – so I stabbed the masking tape with my car key and ripped the box of pictures open like I was gutting a cardboard fish. "*Good enough.*" I kneeled down on the hardwood floor, bent the flaps of the box back, and peered inside. On top was a picture of me and Kyle standing in front of the above-ground pool in the backyard of our house on Lopatcong Drive; we lived there until I was five or so.

I was about four in the picture, so Kyle was seven. We both had more sunburn than freckles, and more gums than teeth in our goofy smiles. I wore a highlighter yellow pool noodle like a boa around my shoulders; I must have been gay even earlier than I thought. Kyle had his arm wrapped my neck, but I didn't see a look of fear in my squinted eyes as if I were worried he'd strangle me. Looking at this picture, one would think these two kids must have gotten along swimmingly, and we did, for the first five or so years, anyway. I remembered how, on one summer afternoon, Kyle saved me from drowning in that pool.

I think it was a weekday, so Mom and Dad were at work and MeeMaw was watching us. She sat in a pool chair on the deck, reading *Country Living* and sipping her homemade iced tea from one of those plastic Camp Snoopy cups from McDonald's. I was splashing happily from the safety of an inflatable octopus, or seahorse, or some kind of ocean creature, while Kyle dove and cannonballed to his heart's content. Suddenly, my trusty sea-dweller capsized, flipping me overboard and sending me to the bottom of our eight-foot-deep pool. As I sank, I saw, through the blurry prism of chlorinated pool water, MeeMaw toss her magazine and iced tea onto the deck and leap from her chair.

She then dove, fully dressed in a floral blouse and creased pair of capris, into the pool to rescue me. She'd recall that, upon reaching the bottom, she couldn't find me. She propelled herself back up to the surface with a single bound from the floor of the pool, and saw me there, sprawled out on the deck and panting for air. Kyle had, without hesitation, jumped into the pool, locked his arms under my armpits, and dragged me to safety. He deposited me onto the deck and sat next to me while MeeMaw, her rouge running and one pearl earring floating in the water behind her, breathed a sigh of relief and shook the water from her de-permed hair.

"I forgot all about that! Thanks, Kyle. And sorry, MeeMaw."

The next picture was taken on my very first birthday. I had absolutely decimated a piece of chocolate cate and smeared the icing all over my face, my bib, my high chair, and my chunky legs. It looked like I had gotten hold of a can of chocolate icing and squeezed it until it popped and exploded all over me. I squealed with delight as MeeMaw posed next to me, pressing her check against my forehead; she wouldn't have been bothered in the slightest if that chocolate had gotten on her. "This has always been my favorite picture of the two of us, MeeMaw."

I flipped past a picture of Frisky: a sweet, ugly cat, affectionately nicknamed "Gremlin" by Dad, that I had rescued from under the porch of an abandoned house on my way home from school. A picture of Kyle and I from some early Halloween. Here I was, the Wicked Witch of the West, and Kyle was Jason Vorhees. He was pretending to cleave the back of my head in the photo. "This picture sums up our relationship pretty well, don't you think?"

Kelly, with a mouthful of braces and wearing a hot pink chiffon frock on her junior prom night. "Yikes! Why do I have this? I guess I can use it for blackmail." Mom and Dad, posing in front of our Christmas tree and also a whole lot of wood paneling. This was back when Mom allowed us to decorate the tree with those terrible ornaments we'd make in school using construction paper, popsicle sticks, and googly eyes. "I hated those ugly things," Mom would later confess. "As soon as you were in middle school I threw all that shit away."

A picture of Dad – he was *definitely* "Goofy" back when this picture was taken – standing in front of his locker at Marine Corps basic training. Times sure were different: I spotted a few packs of cigarettes, some playing cards, a can of beer, and a naked lady pinned up on the inside of his locker door. "Alright, Dad!" He, meanwhile, wore a fittingly goofy grin as he held up a Christmas card from his mother, probably – my Grandma Ellie. She died when I was young, but I remember she was thrilled anytime Dad would bring Kyle and I to visit her, she always had a hard candy in the pocket of her sweater – Grandma Ellie preferred not Werther's Originals, but rather those peppermint candies with the green chocolate swirls – and she had a hearty smoker's chuckle. She'd always get a kick out of our rambunctiousness; Dad would yell "Slow down; don't break anything of your grandmother's!" as we tore through her house, but Grandma Ellie would just clasp her hands in front of her face and laugh. "Oh, Johnny, it's fine," she'd say. "Now, can you pick me up some scratch-offs and Marlboro Reds?"

A picture of Kelly and I at her graduation from boot camp. It's always difficult for me to recall a time when Kelly was taller than me, but here was the proof. She wore her summer whites, crisply pressed, and I wore those jean shorts that came down to the shin and flared out at the bottom; that was the fad back then, don't judge me. Dad pushing me in a stroller in the backyard. He wore a pink and lime green Hawaiian shirt – his favorite, Mom's bane – and I kicked my fat little legs in joy. Oh, I'm eating something; of course I was happy. Kyle and I posing for the first day of school. He leaned as far away from me as possible while just barely touching my shoulder with his pinky. "Get closer to your brother!" I can hear Mom directing us from behind the camera. This is probably when I started to really annoy Kyle and he saw me less as a swimming buddy and more of a nuisance.

Ah, here it is: my favorite picture of all time. It was taken at a get-together at our house. Mom had inexplicably decided on a Hawaiian luau theme for the Fourth of July party. Anyway, Dad was thrilled because he'd get to wear his favorite Hawaiian shirt without provoking Mom's ire. After the hot dogs were devoured but before the star-spangled cupcakes were served, I snuck inside with a balloon in each hand. I put a lei around my neck, donned Dad's straw hat, grabbed fistfuls of sprigs from the vase of flowers on the dining room table, and stuffed the balloons under my shirt to give myself big boobies. I then returned to the backyard to entertain my captive audience with an authentic hula dance complete with the shimmying of an inflated bosom. My routine killed, after the discomfort of seeing a six-year-old boy dressed in full drag as a busty hula girl had subsided, of course. Kelly always cites this as the exact moment she realized her little brother was gay. Mom, meanwhile, cheered on my hip-swaying and preserved this iconic moment for posterity.

"One last thing, Mr. Zalinsky. Where do you want this?"

"Oh, yeah, that." It was the worn, faded poster I'd stumbled upon in some random little record store in a hidden corner of Juffair. The shop owner had been using it to hide a patch of water damage and thought I was joking when I asked "How much?"

"Who's this, John Lennon?"

"Yeah…John Lennon."

"Wow, you must be a big fan. This is a *huge* picture of his face."

"I know. It's so obnoxious, isn't it?"

I didn't hang the poster directly across from my bed like Kyle had; I refuse to wake up every morning to the humongous, looming face of John Lennon. Instead, I hung him up in the tight entranceway to my apartment, partially concealed by the coatrack. I see John every time I leave my place, and every time I come home and hang up my coat. He's unavoidable at those two specific times, but at least not *all* the time. That poster is just one of the thousands of separate, disparate things which remind me of Kyle. He is everywhere; everything in my life has become associated with Kyle, no matter how tiny or far-fetched the connection. He is every song, every piece of Beatles memorabilia, every dirty joke, every painting of the beach, every print of *Washington Crossing the Delaware*, every Seventies *Playboy* cover, every kid with freckles on his nose, every hooptee sputtering down the road, every laugh, every heartbreak.

Chapter 21:
Closure, or Something Close

"Okay, Honey, so tell me all about this Carson!" Mom's eyes lit up, and I secretly found it adorable to see her so interested in my personal life.

"But let's not get too personal here, Mom."

It was a Sunday afternoon; Kelly had invited Mom and I over to her house for no reason in particular. The three of us were drinking coffee and catching up in the living room, while Jameson, Kelly's husband, hid downstairs in his man cave and watched golf.

"Well, I met him downtown once, when I went out," I told Mom. She smiled wide and raised her eyebrows, obviously anticipating more details. "And...he's a really nice guy, and he has cool tattoos, and he can actually hold a conversation."

"Okay, but what about a sense of humor? He'll need a sense of humor to make it in this family!"

"Mom, we're not getting married!" Leave it to Mom to go from zero to wedding in three-point-five seconds.

"Oh, I know, I know. You just always have to keep that in mind. And maybe you *will* get married one day, and then you'll adopt a—"

"Kelly, weren't you just talking about having more kids?"

"Nice try, Kevin, but you're on the hook from now on. I've already given her four grandkids."

"Four grand*sons,* whom I love dearly, but I'd love a cute little granddaughter. You know, like that Lily on *Modern Family!*"

"Geez, Mom...I'll see what I can do, but give me a few years, okay?"

"No rush, Honey! Well…maybe a little rush; I'm getting old. Speaking of *old*," Mom said as she dug for something in her purse next to her on the couch, "Your sister thought she was being funny and gave me *these* when I walked through the door."

"Oh, Kelly…" I shook my head as I scanned the pamphlets for Life Alert and assisted living homes that Mom had thrown on the coffee table.

"What? It's a joke!" Kelly took a sip of coffee to hide her shit-eating grin. "You *just* said you need a sense of humor in this family!"

"Yeah, yeah." Mom playfully kicked Kelly's knee. "You're just *hilarious*."

"How has therapy been going, by the way?" Kelly took another sip of coffee and turned her attention towards me.

"It's going well…I guess. The VA finally got me an appointment."

Kelly tutted. "It's only taken them four months," she sarcastically noted.

"Yeah, but…I guess I'm glad that I'm going. So far, my therapist has been pretty cool. We've talked about Dad, and Kyle, and…other stuff."

"What kind of other stuff?" The lower half of Mom's face might have been concealed by a coffee mug, but those eyebrows fully revealed her skepticism.

"You're not supposed to ask that, Mom!" Kelly flung up a hand in exasperation.

"What?" Mom asked, feigning ignorance. "I'm not supposed to ask what my Honey talks about in therapy?"

"Not really, Mom. But don't worry: it has nothing to do with *you*," I assured her. I think I had an idea of what bothered Mom about my going to therapy.

"Those therapists and psychologists – they always blame the mother!" Bingo. "And I don't know, Honey...I just don't think you need to go to therapy."

"Relax, Mom. I don't blame you for anything. It's just— We've been through a lot in this family, and...I think I've put off dealing with it for too long."

"Well *I*, for one, am proud of you," Kelly smugly declared, eliciting an epic eyeroll from Mom. "You have to take care of yourself, Kevin. Especially now, after leaving the military; that's a big life change."

"I know. And I'm ready to focus on taking care of myself."

"I'm happy for you, Honey. If this is what you want...then I guess I can be okay with it."

"Mom, why is it so much harder for you to accept that I'm in therapy than it was to accept that I'm a gay alcoholic?" I joked, prompting both Mom and Kelly to spit their coffee out into their mugs.

"Don't be fresh!" Mom laughed, wiping the coffee off her chin with a napkin. "I *do* accept it, I do! I'm glad that you're taking care of yourself, Honey."

"Thanks, Mom. I mean, I just started, so we'll see how things go."

"Yes, we *certainly* will," Kelly said in a cryptic tone while flashing me her patented Mom Look. "I will physically drag you to those appointments if I have to."

"Calm down! I'll keep going." I had once witnessed my sister drag Matthew, my oldest nephew, out of the backseat of her car – *through the window* – when he refused to voluntarily get out and take the driving test he'd been putting off for two years. I had not a single doubt in my mind that Beast would do the same thing to me, all in the name of sisterly love. "I have an appointment scheduled for next week. No more four-month waits...hopefully."

"Hi, Uncle Kevin. Hi, MeMe," my second-oldest nephew, Nathan, yelled down to me and Mom from upstairs. He must have been taking a quick break from his computer game to use the bathroom.

"Hi, Nathan!" I yelled back. He's a great kid: responsible, disciplined, organized, stoic…everything I hope to be when *I* grow up.

"Hi, Sweetheart!" Mom called up in her sweetest MeMe voice before turning back to her kids. "Can you believe that shit with that stupid homeowners' association? I mean, that guy let his dog shit all over my lawn without cleaning up after it, and *I* get a warning?"

"Language, MeMe!" Captain Jacob of the Profanity Police, along with his twin brother, Lieutenant Greyson, had scrambled into the house from the backyard for a juice break. The two couldn't possibly be any different, aside from their shared loathing of bad words: Jacob is sassy, and Greyson is sweet; Jacob is a wiz with a Bunsen burner, and Greyson has the best footwork skills on the pee-wee soccer team; Jacob gets infuriated if his reading time is disturbed by so much as a cough, and Greyson will talk until your ears go numb or you retreat into the bathroom and hide in the tub, whichever happens first. They both consistently brighten my mood, and I love Yin and Yang dearly.

"Oh, sorry, Honey! I'll be more careful," Mom promised. My youngest nephews jabbed the straws into their juice boxes and raced back outside to resume their game of cop and potty mouth. Mom continued, only after we heard the back door slam shut, "But isn't that complete bullshit?"

"Well, what did you— Hold on," Kelly held up a finger as she listened to something intently. After a few seconds, she yelled upstairs, "Nathan? Why did you flush that toilet three times? Did you clog it? Are you okay? Use the plunger if you have to!"

"…God, Mom!" Came my nephew's muffled, mortified reply. He had turned the bathroom fan on to keep either his sounds in or our sounds out, to no avail.

"Kelly, let the boy poop in peace!" I, too, know the great frustration of being part of a family which carries on shouted conversations through closed bathroom doors; the throne has lost all sanctity.

"I don't need him breaking the toilet like you and Kyle used to! Anyway, Mom, what did you write that made your neighbor so upset that he'd report you to the HOA?" Kelly asked.

"Oh, nothing serious. I just told him that if I found shit on my front lawn again, I'd throw it at his house and smear it on the windshield of his car." Mom paused before bursting into hysterical laughter. Kelly and I stared at each other in shock – eerily reminiscent of the Fountain Incident – before breaking down and howling along with Mom.

"Oh, is that all?" I asked sarcastically. "Jesus, Mom!" I was laughing so hard I could barely see through the tears.

"Oh, my God." Kelly dabbed the tears from her own eyes with a napkin. "You're totally getting her, Kevin. You might as well take these pamphlets home with you."

"Oh, that is too funny," Mom sighed as she handed her empty coffee mug to Kelly.

"More coffee?"

"No thanks, Sweetie. I'll take some chardonnay if you have it."

"I suppose it *is* about that time," Kelly conceded, standing up from her seat on the couch next to Mom. "Kev?"

I shook my head no. "I guess if I'm going to an Alcoholics Anonymous meeting, my breath probably shouldn't smell like wine."

"Good call," Kelly said as she passed, grabbing my empty cup from the coffee table. "I'll get you some more; the coffee at those meetings is terrible, right?"

"Yeah, and thanks. I think I have time for one more cup." Carson would be picking me up in about fifteen minutes; we were going on our fourth date since reconnecting on Tinder. An Alcoholics Anonymous meeting followed by dinner at the bowling alley...swoon! I just might hit that fifty-seven year mark, after all.

"Oh! Before you go on your date, Honey," Mom said, waving her hand at me to grab my full attention. "I talked to your sister, and...I think I'm ready to look at the death certificate."

"You are? You don't mean...Kyle's death certificate?" Mom nodded her head as I struggled to resist the urge to shake mine. Kelly returned from the kitchen with a cup of coffee for me and a glass of wine for Mom. "Kelly, what do you think?"

"Well, it's been eight years. If Mom thinks she's ready..." Kelly trailed off as she went back into the kitchen. She returned after a few seconds with her own glass of wine. "We can't keep her from seeing it."

"I know, but are you sure she—"

"Now, hold on, you two. *She* is sitting right here," Mom sternly reminded us, glancing back and forth between me and Kelly. "And I'm ready. Let me see it, Kelly."

"Okay, okay, if you're sure. I'll go grab it," Kelly said as she made her way towards the stairs with more than a little hesitation. "You're *sure* you're sure?"

Mom nodded assuredly before taking a hearty swig of chardonnay. Mom is the toughest person I know, besting even her Airport Incident collaborator, but even so: I wasn't entirely convinced that she'd steeled her nerves enough to handle seeing the cause of her son's death written in black and white. Mom would often wonder aloud if Kyle's death was just an unfortunately fatal accident, prompting Kelly and I to go silent and avoid eye contact for fear of entering into a discussion from which there could be no clean escape.

"Okay, Mom," Kelly sighed as she descended from upstairs with a folded stack of stapled papers. "Here it is. But I have to warn you – it's very clinical and matter-of-fact."

"I *think* I can handle it, Kelly. I've only been in the medical field for a hundred years. Plus…I already know what it's going to say." Kelly handed Mom the document with a faint grimace; she and I exchanged a nervous look as Mom unfolded the papers. She spent the next few minutes scanning each page, flipping it over, scanning the flipside, flipping it back over, and re-examining the front before moving on. Her eyebrows were narrowed intently and her mouth was twisted into a pursed, pensive expression. "Here it is," she sighed, after what must have been fifteen minutes.

"You found it?" Kelly asked nervously, peering over the top of the page Mom was currently opened to.

"Yep. Probable cause of death: suicide." Mom gently tossed the stack of papers onto the coffee table and looked up at us; we had been holding our breath and staring at her for the entirety of those fifteen minutes. "Breathe, you two! I don't need to lose any more of my kids! I told you: I already knew what it was going to say."

"And…how do you feel about it?" I asked, moving to sit next to Mom on the sofa as I spoke. Kelly returned to her seat on Mom's other side.

"I feel…okay," Mom replied, sinking back into the couch and folding her hands in her lap. "I feel okay." She took a deep breath and let loose a huge sigh, and the tension was sucked clean out of the room. Her eyes were welling not with tears, nor with hurt, nor with sadness, but with something unexpected and beautiful: relief. "It's been a really tough…hell, twelve years. But I have you – *both of you*, Kelly, not just 'the Favorite' – and my grandkids, so I'm okay…Now, *please* stop looking at me like I have lobsters crawling out of my nose!"

"Love you, Mom," Kelly said, in probably the sweetest voice I had ever heard come out of her mouth, as she pressed herself against Mom's shoulder; Mom reared her head back in shock.

"Where did *that* come from?" Mom snorted as she reached for her half-empty glass of wine on the coffee table.

"What? I'm capable of expressing love for my own mother, you know! I'm not a monster."

"No, no, of course not, Sweetie. You're...*a beast!*" Mom threw her hand up for a high five and I happily obliged.

"You got that from Kevin, didn't you?" Kelly glared at me in mock offense, stifling her laughter.

"Sorry! But when you fly through the air and knock someone to the ground – and then bash his face against the floor until his *braces get stuck in the carpet* – you're gonna earn yourself a nickname!"

"Ha! I forgot all about that! Do you remember how Dad had to cut Kyle free with scissors?"

"Don't forget about the bloodstains you left all over the carpet! It took me *days* to get that shit out!"

"Mom, that wasn't really Kelly's fault..."

"How about the time Kyle and I flipped the couch over and Max bit me on the ass?"

"Oh, I loved that couch! You kids ruined everything. That's exactly why—"

"You kids are the reason why we don't have nice things!" Kelly and I flawlessly imitated Mom in unison, and we all cracked up.

"Well, it's *true!* Something was always getting destroyed in our house. How about when your brother kicked out the porch window?"

"And the poor Chinese delivery guy was so scared, he dropped our food! I was just glad my sweet and sour chicken survived."

"I still can't believe we were *actually* banned from that restaurant! And...sorry again that we ruined your big night, Kev."

"Oh, it's okay. I was just glad it wasn't *me* who was trapped under the couch with Kyle. The closet was a much safer place."

"No more 'closet' for you, Honey! I'm just so happy that you met someone sweet…"

"Brace yourself, Kevin."

"…who you just *might* marry one day, and then—"

"And then you'd get your Lily. I know, Mom, I know. Just…let me work on one thing at a time, please."

"Okay, Honey. You just take your time."

Thank You

I didn't have to use my imagination very much when writing this book, since these events are a *lightly fictionalized* account of my own life. I changed everybody's name except for those of myself and my immediate family. If you read this book and come across a character who you think might have been inspired by you, please don't sue me. Be proud of yourself! For you have impacted my life in such a meaningful way that I was inspired to rearrange the letters of your name – or just change the first letter of your name – and pay tribute to you in this, my humble life story. So *thank you*; I really mean it.

Thank you, Mom, for being the backbone of this family and also the single funniest person I have known, do know, and ever will know. I love you, and I don't think I can adequately express just how much I appreciate you.

Thank you, Kelly, for being my rock in hard times and my friend in all times. You were my very first role model, and not just because you'd beat Kyle up when he was being a total jerk to me. I love you.

Thank you, Dad, for being such a huge influence on the way I conduct myself as a human being, including in this very moment, so many years after your passing. I love you, and I miss you so much.

Thank you, Kyle, for being the yin to my yang, for balancing my spirit and my energy, and for helping me realize that to be different from others is not a weakness or a defect, but a gift. I love you, and I miss you.

Thank you, Uncle Tom (or Uncle Tim), for jokingly responding "That's a good title for a book!" when I answered your question with "I'm still working on it." I love you.

And *thank you* for reading this book. I hope it made you laugh, made you feel good, made you feel *something*, or even just made you smile.

Made in the USA
Middletown, DE
12 July 2018